COUNTRY SCRAPPLE

Also by William Woys Weaver

Encyclopedia of Food and Culture
Sauer's Herbal Cures
100 Vegetables and Where They Came From
Food and Drink in Medieval Poland
Heirloom Vegetable Gardening
Pennsylvania Dutch Country Cooking
The Christmas Cook
America Eats
Thirty-Five Receipts
Sauerkraut Yankees
A Quaker Woman's Cookbook

COUNTRY SCRAPPLE

An American Tradition

William Woys Weaver

Illustrations by
Signe Sundberg-Hall

Foreword by
Chef Fritz Blank
Deux Cheminées, Philadelphia

STACKPOLE
BOOKS

Published by
STACKPOLE BOOKS
5067 Ritter Road
Mechanicsburg, PA 17055
www.stackpolebooks.com

Printed in the United States of America

10 9 8 7 6 5 4 3 2 1

FIRST EDITION

Design by Beth Oberholtzer

Library of Congress Cataloging-in-Publication Data

Weaver, William Woys, 1947–
     Country scrapple : an American tradition / William Woys Weaver ;
  illustrations by Signe Sundberg-Hall ; foreword by Fritz Blank.–1st ed.
       p.   cm.
  Includes bibliographical references and index.
  ISBN 0-8117-0064-X
  1. Cookery (Meat)   I. Title.
TX749.W36   2003
641.6′6–dc21

2003008248

In memory of Susan Lucas (1949–2001)
Whose untimely death deprived us of a living legend.

CONTENTS

FOREWORD

As an advocate, consumer, and defender of the food called scrapple, it is with great pleasure that I write the foreword to this book. My first food memories are of Sunday breakfasts with eggs, toast, homemade jellies and jams—especially fox grape—and wonderful, crispy scrapple, pan-fried in lard. With this often came a side offering of Victory Garden spring scallions, served raw and dipped into small piles of salt. As part of my family's German heritage, scrapple was eaten with pleasure, plain or with maple syrup or black strap molasses or catsup. We also ate scrapple for dinner, which is what we called lunch, and our evening meal, which we called supper.

Later in life, I discovered many of the various guises scrapple takes and am particularly fond of puddin' meat, a loose mush that I first encountered when I worked at a dairy cattle dispersal sale on the eastern shore of Maryland. I also recall watching scrapple being made in a cook tent at the Pennsylvania Dutch Folk Festival in Kutztown, Pennsylvania. I was mesmerized by an Old Order Amish woman who fished a whole pig's liver out of a simmering cauldron with a long-handled, two-pronged fork and sliced the steaming meat carefully. She ate it with just a pinch of salt and great gusto, savoring it with such relish that I yearned to taste it then and there.

Often misunderstood, scrapple needs to be exonerated. Over the years, people have taunted me for eating such a nasty dish. They had been taught that scrapple is made from the eyeballs and unmentionable orifices of hogs. "Nasty, nasty stuff," they would hiss. These admonitions were almost convincing given some of my experiences with scrapple in shabby truck stops. On occasion, I have been served something that on the menu was called scrapple, but which was hard, greasy shingles, having been cast in fry-o-laters full of dark, very old oil, reeking of fish and whatever else had been assaulted in those catchall pools of near-rancid fat. Thank goodness for other memories of excellent scrapple cooked properly.

So, it is with these memories that I read this wonderful work. Indeed, William Woys Weaver has exonerated this great American culinary tradition. He is an aficionado of scrapple in all of its forms—panhas, goetta, puddin' meat—as am I.

Scrapple is simply "wonderful good."

Fritz Blank
Chef de Cuisine et Propriétaire
Deux Cheminées, Philadelphia

ACKNOWLEDGMENTS

As with every book of this kind, there are a great number of people whose help behind the scenes made invaluable contributions to this project. First of all, I would like to thank Dr. Don Yoder, Professor Emeritus of the University of Pennsylvania, for his constant advice on all matters dealing with the history of scrapple, his willingness to call up a number of scrapple makers on my behalf (he speaks fluent *Pennsylfaanisch*), and his Olympian appetite during tasting sessions. John T. Edge of the Southern Foodways Alliance (University of Mississippi) was extremely helpful with advice and materials dealing with liver mush. Johanna Maria van Winter, University of Utrecht (Netherlands), must be thanked heartily for help with medieval sources. Likewise, Johannes van Dam, Dutch food historian and expert on *balkenbrij*, also shared with me many valuable insights into the Dutch counterparts to American scrapple. Jon Christensen, restaurant and wine reviewer of the *Columbus Dispatch*, gave me many helpful tips on Ohio scrapple makers. And Doreen Howard proved to be a bridge into the world of the Choctaw and Chickasaw; it was Doreen who connected me with *pashofa*.

Regarding the recipes, Verna Dietrich of Dietrich's Meats in Krumsville, Pennsylvania, provided very helpful advice on scrapple making and terminology. Margaret Lauterbach of Boise, Idaho, kindly allowed me to record her family's story about venison scrapple, as did L. Wilbur Zimmerman with his wonderful recipe for oldtime ham scrapple. I also thank those generous recipe contributors who requested to remain anonymous; their privacy has been respected. My crew of recipe tasters, including Dorene Pasekoff, Frank Desimone, and a slew of Mennonite long-distance runners (Mike Clemmer and Ron Beidler among them), all provided honest, off-the-cuff comments that were much more valuable than they realized.

Naturally, I also want to thank my patient editor, Kyle Weaver, for encouraging me to write this book—the concept changed dramatically from our first brainstorming sessions, and much for the better. I want to thank chef Fritz Blank of Deux Cheminées in Philadelphia for his personal interest in the project and for his valuable comments in the foreword. My dear friend, artist Signe Sundberg-Hall, has supplied more wonderful drawings; this is the fourth book she has illustrated for me. Then of course I must thank my literary agent, Blanche Schlessinger, whose fighting spirit has brought her back from death's door; through her example, she has taught me how to focus on the things in life that count most.

This brings me to Susan Lucas, my longtime friend who died tragically before she was able to enjoy the fruits of all that butchering she used to do on behalf of hands-on food history. Sue supplied the squirrels when I needed them, brought the venison down from the mountains, and even ground the corn at historic Newlin's Mill in Delaware County, Pennsylvania, so that I would have enough old-style cornmeal to make scrapple for an army. She drove a truck but wore handmade eighteenth-century clothes, and fit the part to a tee. I have dedicated this book to her because she certainly earned it. She would also be pleased to know that in a sense, she was cooking from the grave every time I tested a recipe. The venison is gone now, but there is still enough cornmeal left to write another book.

Scrapple:
An Introduction

For many Americans, scrapple evokes an image of overalls and hot coffee, of Formica tables at a truck-stop breakfast steaming under the neon glare of a stainless steel diner. There is no denying that scrapple is now firmly ensconced on the menus of breakfast palaces dotting the crossroads of rural America. But scrapple is also a recording label, a jazz band from New Zealand, a 1998 movie, and the theme of a famous bebop tune by the late saxophonist Charlie "Bird" Parker. Scrapple is all of this and more. It is a working man's dish with ancient genealogy tracing back to pork gruel and a leap of pioneer ingenuity that christened it with the name scrapple several centuries ago. It all happened in Philadelphia, and the evolution from cooking scrapple on a hoe blade to serving it up on turn-of-the-century silver is only part of a long, fascinating story about a food that has earned itself a permanent place in the history of American cookery.

For the uninitiated, scrapple is a mixture of meat and flour cooked in meat stock until it thickens. It is allowed to stiffen and set like Italian polenta, then is sliced and fried in a skillet until brown and crispy on both sides. Scrapple is an old breakfast dish that has become a symbol of early American cookery as well as a cultural bridge between the Old World and New.

There are many types of scrapple, each with its own regional character and local name. The most famous of these is Philadelphia scrapple, or buckwheat scrapple, which traces its origin to northwest Germany. The most unusual old-style scrapple is the scrabbling mush

1

*Pennsylvania Dutch
"scrapple palace"
at Palmyra, 1959.*

of the Carolina coast, which is made with rice. On the other hand, what is unusual? Groundhog scrapple? A recipe exists. Buffalo scrapple? Native Americans eat it. Nut scrapple? Vegetarians swear by it. Apple scrapple? You missed the cooking demo on "Good Morning America."

The finer points of Philadelphia scrapple were first taught to me as a small child. It was something I ate at my grandmother's house. That and freshly baked cinnamon buns were the highlights of her breakfasts. She cooked the scrapple in large, black, cast-iron skillets, her grandmother Hannum's, in fact, cast at the old Philadelphia foundry of Savery & Company, well seasoned and smooth. I still have Susan Darlington Hannum's skillets, and I treasure them: four generations of loving use, four generations of anointment by scrapple.

I am fairly certain that Susan Hannum prepared her own home-made scrapple, because there were pigs on her farm at Dugdale near Red Lion, Pennsylvania, just as there were pigs on the Pocopson farm in Chester County where my grandmother grew up. In fact, my grandmother's father, William Ellesworth Hickman, owned a pork butchering business, and the scrapple he sold at the West Chester, Pennsylvania, farmers' market was at one time a well-known local product. I never had the pleasure of eating that scrapple, because the Hickmans had sold their business long before I was born. The scrapple I remember was Strode's, made out in the country at Strode's Mill in Chester County, Pennsylvania. It was processed in a small, eighteenth-century stone mill set picturesquely along a creek. My grandmother would drive there to get it. She knew the owners (they were distantly related) and trusted their recipe because it tasted like her father's scrapple. It also came with the all-important thin layer of white fat on the top.

In the days before vacuum packaging, very clean rendered pork fat was poured on top of each pan of scrapple to seal it, the way many country patés are still prepared in France; the French call that rendered fat *saindoux*. This feature inevitably became the bottom when the scrapple was turned out, wrapped, and sold. That fat was lightly brushed over the cooking pan once the iron was hot, just enough to make the bottom appear wet. When the skillet began to smoke, the heat was turned down very low and the sliced scrapple added. The smell of herbs, especially sage, soon permeated the kitchen.

When my grandmother cooked scrapple, it came to the table on large china platters, and it was quite common for our family to go through one or two pints of scrapple sauce in one sitting. Scrapple sauce is whatever you like to eat with scrapple; for us, it was usually some kind of pepper hash or green tomato relish. Scrapple seems to require a condiment, and many people think tomato catsup is contrast enough, but it is not. The modern kind is too red and much too sweet. Scrapple is a high-energy country dish for hard-working farmers; there is no need to garnish it with sugar, although it is rumored that some people think molasses is better than catsup, and that maple syrup is even better than molasses. But from a nutritional standpoint, the sour condiments are much healthier.

The very thought of molasses or syrup on scrapple made my grandmother scowl. The combination seemed to her sacrilegious. There was a certain etiquette involved with eating scrapple, and to her molasses crossed over the line. Such unwritten rules as that remind me of the Clement Allen scrapple advertisements in the *Friends' Intelligencer* before World War I. A waiter looking very much like a medieval page was depicted coming toward the viewer with a large silver tray covered with smoking slices of Allen scrapple. A silver breakfast service for scrapple? Only in Baltimore or Philadelphia.

The feature that makes scrapple special no matter how it is served is that it seems to define something essentially regional and essentially American. It is one of those down-home foods that set us apart from the rest of the postindustrial world. Is it any wonder that many Native Americans make it? The recipe for Potawatomi Beef Scrapple from Oklahoma (page 98) is just one case in point.

I never realized years ago, when I was interviewed by Leslie Land for an article on scrapple in the *New York Times,* that I would end up writing this history of scrapple and its many variant forms. Anyone else would have said it was inevitable. Both of my paternal great-grandfathers made scrapple, and my grandmother's father was the junior partner in a small butchering firm once known as Joseph P. Hickman & Son. They were old-time country pork butchers. Pigs were their stock and trade. They owned a stall at the first Reading Terminal Market in Philadelphia (the second market is the one standing today).

Pigs still run in my blood, but in a very different way. They fascinate me because they are primitive. Their primeval behavior elevated them among pagan deities, and the foods made from them were invested with ancient meanings associated with the seasonal cycles of planting and harvest. Some of this lies at the historical roots of scrapple. In all honesty, this is one of the first books to tackle the subject, to go back to the ancient origins, and then follow the evolutionary trail up to the present. Scrapple has its detractors; it is a love-it-or-leave-it sort of food. But there are two things that no one can deny: Scrapple is firmly embedded in American culinary tradition, and its point of introduction into our cookery occurred several centuries ago in the general area of the Delaware Valley.

Aside from being a history, this is also a cookbook. There are two types of recipes. Some, included in sidebars verbatim as originally written, are provided as historical evidence, some more easy to reproduce than others. An entire chapter is devoted to recipes that have been tested for today's home kitchen. Scrapple was not originally a kitchen preparation; it was a by-product of butchering made outside or in a special outdoor shed. But over the past 150 years, the whole process has been downsized in cookbook literature to the kind of small-batch cookery that allows you to make scrapple with little trouble and a minimum of ingredients. In addition to easy-to-make scrapple recipes, I have also included a recipe for Pennsylvania Dutch *Metzelsupp* (butchering-day stew), a wintertime classic, as well as a few recipes for scrapple sauces, because scrapple is best not eaten alone.

My recipes for scrapple ought to underline that much of what is disliked about the dish is in the mind of the beholder: Hot dogs and fast-food hamburgers contain far more frightening ingredients. Change the name to *polenta nera* (black polenta, or polenta made with buckwheat), and you can sell scrapple at any upscale restaurant. But no matter what you call it, scrapple is scrapple, as its original dialect name signifies: a mush cake, a slice of pot pudding fried on the blade of a grubbing hoe. By pedigree, it is early American; by its very nature, it is rustic. Most important, scrapple is a lasting symbol of hardy endurance, having survived all the major shifts in taste that have transformed American cooking over the past three hundred years.

The European Origins of Scrapple

By a quirk of fate, I managed to acquire a house that was once a tavern. The house has gained a certain degree of recognition due to its status as a National Register building, but for me its long-demolished kitchens remain one of its most fascinating puzzles. The tavern was licensed in 1812 to Philadelphia beef butcher (and Revolutionary War hero) George Rees and called The Lamb, but I am not certain lamb was served there. Scrapple was. A large piggery stood near a log barn in the 1820s, and when farmers drove hogs and cattle into Philadelphia from nearby counties, the animals were allowed to bed down for the night in one of the fields belonging to The Lamb. The drovers brought their own mattresses and quilts, but it was the wife of the tavern keeper—Maria Clinger, to be exact—who cooked their breakfasts of sliced onions and scrapple, buckwheat cakes, cottage cheese well flavored with chives, and apple butter for the freshly baked bread. Drovers were the lowlifes of rural culture in those days. They ate their meals from sturdy English ironstone and drank gin slings by the pint.

Scrapple was part of this daily cycle, a vignette of meals repeated thousands of times throughout the Mid-Atlantic region during the nineteenth century. No one butchered a pig specifically to make scrapple, just as no one ate scrapple as a main meal course. Scrapple was a by-product, a frugal culinary solution for dealing with leftover butchering broth. It was always eaten along with other foods, and only during the cold months of the year. Scrapple is known in differ-

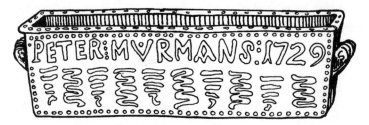

Slip-decorated redware pan for Westphalian Panhas from Kamperbrück near Crefeld, Germany. The inscription reads "Peter Murmans 1729."

ent places by different names. The Pennsylvania Dutch call it *Panhas;* Philadelphians call it scrapple; people in rural Maryland, Virginia, and North Carolina call it liver mush; many southerners call it scraffle or poor-do. These conflicting terminologies are a reflection of the fact that several closely related culinary traditions have merged into one on American soil. The roots of these traditions trace back to pre-Roman Europe, particularly to the Europe once inhabited by Celtic-speaking peoples—both on the Continent and in the British Isles.

The antiquity of scrapple is attested to by its most ancient name: *pannas,* which is generally written in modern German as *Panhas.* This spelling is also used in *Pennsylfaanisch,* the language of the Pennsylvania Dutch. It survives in modern French as *panne,* unrendered hog's lard. Celtic linguist Pierre-Yves Lambert has pointed out in *La langue gauloise* (The Gaulish Language) that *panna* is a pot or pan in the Celtic spoken by the ancient Gauls.[1] Swiss historian Christian Holliger has also noted that the word *panna* appears as graffiti on large, Gaulish-manufactured terra sigillata serving bowls, thus suggesting that the term *panna* may have covered a range of utensils.[2] It is also quite possible that the graffiti meant something else: that these bowls were used to serve the hot *pannas* on butchering day. It would be interesting to study the terra sigillata decorative motifs in this light. It is clear, however, that *pannas* derived its name from the utensil in which it was cooked rather than from a specific ingredient. Its original meaning was probably very similar to what is meant by scrapple today: a generic word for pot pudding, a meaty gruel allowed to set or stiffen in a pan or bowl. Linguists have argued that since the Germans borrowed the term from their Gaulish neighbors, they must not have had a word for it themselves. In this respect, scrapple may represent a dish of extraordinary continuity, a highly ritualized cultural artifact adopted by the Germans who settled among the Gauls during the Roman period.

Yet while certain features remained the same, this continuity from one culture to the next was also accompanied by change. The survival of scrapple over so many millennia has been predicated on the ability of its makers to adapt when confronted with new ingredients, new food habits, and evolving social contexts. However, at the base of its most ancient roots lies the idea of ritual slaughter, as Patrice Méniel has so ably explored in *Les gauloise et les animaux* (The Gauls and Animals). Indeed, in the Celtic context, the ritual slaughter of pigs was doubtless sacrificial in nature and bound up with notions about the underworld, death, and annual renewal. Archeological evidence from a late Neolithic site at Durrington Walls in England points to an annual gathering observed by Celtic peoples specifically for the slaughter and consumption of pork.[3]

The logical conclusion would be to connect this annual pork cookout with one of two Celtic feasts: Lughnasa, the great August market fair presided over by the god Lugh or Lugus, or Samain, the calendrical observation of the Celtic New Year on the eve of November 1. Both were major feast days throughout Celtic Europe, and there is considerable lore connecting pigs to the menus.[4] In the case of Lughnasa, there is a direct association with the swine god Moccus, whose name is based on the Celtic word for pig (*moch* in Welsh). This term survives in English as *muck* (where pigs wallow).

On the other hand, since Lughnasa fell more or less at the height of summer (August 1), the hot weather would argue against scrapple as a significant feature. Pit roasting of whole animals seems to have been the summer pattern. Fall butchering is a more likely terminus, since this was also the time of year when bacon, hams, and sausages were prepared. In short, the farmer was not celebrating a good harvest thanks to Lugh; rather, he was looking toward the dark days of winter and enough provisioning to survive until spring. Scrapple was part of this survival strategy.

The pig of highest rank in ancient times was the wild boar, a favorite cult animal among the Celts, especially the nobility, which devoted itself to the hunt. Arduinna was a boar goddess in the Ardennes Forest of France, and perhaps most significantly for Samain, boars are often depicted attending upon Cernunnos, a horned god connected with the underworld. It was during Samain that the underworld opened,

Marble pig, 350–330 B.C., from the temnos of Demeter at Knidos, Greece.
BRITISH MUSEUM

time stood still, and the dead made contact with the living. This association of pigs with the underworld is also present in Greek mythology, for it was Eubouleos the swineherd who became a priest of the Mysteries of Demeter (Mother Earth) at Eleusis in Attika after seeing Persephone taken into the underworld. Since his pigs were said to have fallen into the great hole where Persephone disappeared, pigs were the most common sacrificial offering in the chthonic rituals of Demeter and Persephone. Many images surviving from antiquity, like the one shown above, attest to this.

Whatever the original mythic significance, pork persisted as a symbol of fall butchering in preparation for winter throughout the Middle Ages and even into the early twentieth century. Among the ancient Gauls, the meat was ritually divided according to social hierarchy, the best cuts going to the most powerful individuals. Meat-flavored gruel was distributed to the masses. This pattern passed into medieval culture, where the villagers who helped with the butchering were rewarded with meat or sausages as well as a bowl of butcher's stew, a gruel made from the remains of the butchering process thickened with meal. This gruel became scrapple when it was allowed to thicken and set like a pudding. The festive nature of butchering day was thus prolonged for a week, or for as long as the scrapple held out. Gruels of this type were made all over Europe during the butchering season, although local conditions, such as the available grain, determined the character of the recipes. Furthermore, there were two ways to transform the broth: boil it with meal or flour, or bake it. This technical difference gave rise to two distinct types of scrapple: the polenta-like dish we know today, and the baked meat pâtés that are now commonly associated with French cookery. During the Middle Ages, both types of scrapple were prepared in most regions of Europe, although they varied widely in composition and flavor. But one rule prevailed: The more meat in the dish, the richer the protein and fat content, the higher its status.

The White Broth, the Black Pudding

Since scrapple is impossible to make without a broth, the broth is its fundamental ingredient from both a structural and psychological viewpoint. This critical issue has surfaced many times in my conversations with modern scrapple makers. For example, Kessler's in Lemoyne, Pennsylvania, uses beef broth instead of pork stock because they prefer what they describe as beef's cleaner palate—it is not so strong tasting as pork. Theirs is a culinary choice, but the fact remains, the central importance of the stock is ancient. This is confirmed again by the work of Pierre-Yves Lambert, who has determined that the terminology and structural concepts regarding the broth are of Celtic origin. One of these terms is *bouillon-blanc,* a word now commonly used in French for white stock, but in its ancient meaning, it referred to both *Verbascum phlomoides,* an herb known in English as orange mullein, and a broth flavored or

Orange mullein (Verbascum phlomoides), *the bouillon-blanc of medieval France. From a sixteenth-century woodcut.* ROUGHWOOD COLLECTION

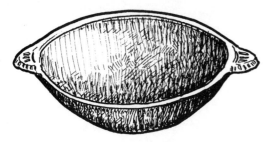

The Scottish quaich, or drinking vessel, was used for sipping the ritual broth and ritual gruels. Its design is based on the ancient condy, which is often depicted in the hand of the god Lugh in Gaulish art. This example dates from about 1780. ROUGHWOOD COLLECTION

thickened with it.[5] The flowers of this plant are a rich source of saponines and create a slimy texture similarly to okra. They were used by the Gauls in cookery much the way gumbo filé is used in American Cajun cooking. Thus there are two types of whiteness in the basic butchering stock.

The first whiteness is the stock itself, the color of pork broth created by boiling bones and leftover bits of meat. By drinking it, the consumer was once believed to acquire certain attributes of the pig (fecundity, sexual strength, heroic fighting abilities), as it represented the extracted essence of the animal. This idea of potency survives in the Westphalian folk remedy *fehlt de Hoor op'n Kopp, schmer Pannhas drop* (for a balding head, smear it with scrapple). In other words, it restores male vigor. The mullein added a medical or magical whiteness in that it was considered prophylactic or protective. Primarily, it aided digestion, especially after the consumption of a meal consisting mostly of meat. It is easy to see that one would complement the other during heavy feasting. This use of orange mullein in meat stock persisted into the Middle Ages in the form of home remedies and food for invalids, and herbal additives were a key element in the scrapples that evolved in America. Drinking the broth or white stock may have held significations similar to the drinking of broth at the bull feasts in ancient Scotland. In order to divine during sleep who would become the new king, certain individuals drank the broth from the cauldron as part of the ritual process. Not enough is known about the ritual slaughter of boars and swine among the Celts, but the practice of boiling the animal's liver in the broth and dividing this among those present may suggest an old divination role. This is still done among the Pennsylvania Dutch, who generally consume it with coarse salt. This act of commensality recalls the old practice of breaking bread with neighbors and eating it with salt, a very basic form of communal bonding.

Liver served two functions in scrapple: It was cooked in the white stock, thus flavoring it, or it was broken into the scrapple itself to enrich the gruel. The ancient Romans prized pork liver as a delicacy and force-fed hogs with dried figs to enlarge their livers in the same manner that they enlarged goose livers. The Roman cookery book called *De Re Coquinaria* refers specifically to a recipe employing enlarged pork livers, called *ficatum* in Latin.[6] The Roman and Gaulish preoccupation with livers and entrails was in part linked to ritual butchering. There were probably many types of scrapples now extinct, such as goose scrapple, rabbit scrapple, and goat scrapple, all connected with certain pagan feast days. Some of these ritualistic foods still persist in altered form, such as the *cacen waed gwyddau* (goose blood tart) of Wales.

Another significance of the white stock was that to the Celtic imagination, many of the most potent things were white, such as semen, milk, and the berries of mistletoe. The color was also associated with purity and purification. Red was another potent color, as it represented a different kind of essence: blood. Blood was far more potent than white broth because it was not symbolic or abstract; it was the life substance of the creature from which it was taken. For this reason, it was an important element in all forms of Celtic ritual sacrifice, including that of humans.

Blood played a significant role in the history of scrapple and is one of the traditional ingredients that persists in German scrapple to this day—as well as one of the first ingredients to disappear from Americanized versions of the dish. Medieval English cookery books normally refer to most types of blood-based foods as black puddings, and this blackness was one of the original elements in medieval plum pudding (a dried fruit, blood, and meal mixture). Blood is most familiar to American readers in the form of German *Blutwurst* (blood sausage), but it also appears in a wide range of peasant foods closely related to American scrapple.

Among these is Polish *kiszka*, a blood-and-grain-based sausage. *Kiszka* is nothing more than coarsely textured scrapple boiled in a sausage skin. It is also quite similar to the ancient Celtic *pannas*, using oatmeal or barley meal as a thickener. These were the commonest grains for meat-flavored gruels, but in France, Spain, and parts of what is now southern Germany, the ancient grain of choice was emmer wheat, spelt (a form of emmer wheat), or millet. This difference was determined by climate and soil, and it accounts for the wide range of preparations that have survived from the early Middle Ages. An example of a millet-based scrapple would be Slovenian *šára,* a mixture of millet, white stock, and pork blood baked in the oven in an earthenware vessel.[7] It is cut into pieces when served and is often reheated by frying on a griddle.

Scrapple in the Middle Ages

Aside from medieval pictures depicting fall butchering, there is not much to link these images to scrapple. There are no known pictures of people cooking scrapple, and there are no scrapple recipes in surviving manuscript cookery books from the period. We can only assume that scrapple was one of the several food products being prepared because it was part of the traditional butchering process. But there are many circumstantial clues that have been studied in detail by Dutch ethnographer Hielke van der Meulen. In the Limburg area of the Netherlands, traditional scrapple *(balkenbrij)* is reddish black due to the addition of pork blood; in Brabant, the blood color is imitated with sandalwood, a popular culinary spice during the Middle Ages. Many more useful clues are buried in the small number of medieval butchering recipes that survive, among them a recipe from the 1400s written in a mixture of Dutch and Flemish. It is titled *Om bulinck te maken van vercken op sin Limborchs* (To Make Blood Pudding the Limburg Way) and may be found in the manuscript collection of the Koninklijke Academie voor Nederlandse Taal- en Letterkunde at Ghent, Belgium.[8]

Instead of using oatmeal (or barley flour) and buckwheat flour, Limburg blood pudding was thickened with grated rye bread and white bread soaked in cream. This bread puree also contained the pork blood, a generous measure of raw suet, cream, pepper, onion, and saffron. It was then stuffed into a gut. Country scrapple was never made with such elaborate ingredients, a clear indication that the Limburg blood pudding was some type of festive dish for the well-to-do.

Wild boar from a fifteenth-century woodcut.
ROUGHWOOD COLLECTION

Om bulinck te maken van vercken op sin Limborchs

Dan sult ghij nemen bloet, ende een half kan romen tot eenen ver-cken, ende peperpoeder, ende wat sofferaen, ende [a]iun cleijn gescerft, ende roggenbroot geraspet, ende witbrood in roomen te weijcken geset, ende doer eenen peperdoeck gheslagen, ende salt, dit stamen ondereen gheroert, ende dat vet cleijn gesneden, ende die clierkens uuijtgesneden, ended an die bulinck gevult een wei-jnich meer dan de helft.

To Make Blood Pudding the Limburg Way

Then, for one pig, takest thou the blood, and half a *kan* [1 pint] of cream, and pepper powdered, and a little saffron, and onion chopped small, and rye bread grated, and white bread soaked in cream and strained through a spice cloth, and salt; all of this stirred together, and the suet chopped small, and the membrane cut away, and then the sausage filled to a little more than half.

The translation is courtesy of Dr. Johanna Maria van Winter, Utrecht. A spice cloth is a piece of lawn (a fine linen fabric) used for sifting. The finest lawn in this period was made in Cyprus. The "membrane" in the suet is what becomes cracklings after the fat is rendered. The sausage skin is not filled tight in order that the contents can expand when boiled. After the sausage is boiled, the broth can be thickened for scrapple.

Thus the red *balkenbrij* of Limburg and Brabant is doubtless a farm-house adaptation of this old medieval model: scrapple made to look like blood pudding.

History does repeat itself in other ways, because a number of recent Internet recipes for American scrapple call for sweetened condensed milk instead of meat stock to moisten the dry ingredients. This substitute echoes the cream-and-blood sausages of the Middle Ages and probably takes its cue from old-time chipped-beef gravy preparations, since this modern-day scrapple is made in a skillet rather than boiled thick in a kettle. In any case, everyday food like scrapple never appeared in cookery books in the late Middle Ages because making it was common knowledge; no recipe was required. What good were cookbooks to peasant farmers who could not read or write?

And yet, even medieval nobility ate scrapple. The nobility slaughtered pigs, and noblewomen are known to have made their own sausages, as a circa 1465 letter of Czech noblewoman Anézka od Rožmberk well attests.[9] However, the scrapple they ate was much more elaborate than contemporary peasant preparations and contained such spices as cloves, ginger, and cinnamon; dried fruit; and white bread or wheat flour. In appearance and taste, it was quite different from the simple country dishes we know today. If old-style Westphalian *Panhas* made with pork blood, white stock, bits of meat, barley meal, and buckwheat flour could be equated with a particular class, then it was most certainly food of the wealthy peasant and the very low nobility who lived among the peasants more or less on the same economic level. These are the people whom Pieter Brueghel and his son depicted with such vividness in their paintings from the 1500s. In several of their paintings, butchering is taking place, and all the important implements are arranged according to their function, including large bowls for collecting the blood.

Linguistic evidence proves that the Pennsylvania Dutch term *Panhas* traces to the Lower Rhineland, and that the only immigrants who could have introduced this dialect word were the Crefelder Quakers and Mennonites who settled near Philadelphia in the 1680s. They were also responsible for the early association of the dish with Philadelphia and its culinary culture. At first glance, it would seem that those first thirteen families exerted a disproportionately large influence on the foodways of both the English and German settlers in Pennsylvania. On the other hand, they settled in a close-knit community in Germantown, and it was through this village overlooking Philadelphia that the Germans living in the interior passed back and forth for the Wednesday and Saturday markets. In a very real sense, Germantown served as a cultural crossroad between German- and English-speaking Pennsylvania, and it was here that the extremely important Sauer press was established in the late 1730s. With that, Germantown became the center of German book printing in colonial America.

The early records of Philadelphia are mostly silent on the subject of scrapple because the word did not come into general speech until the 1800s. Prior to that time, the dish was often referred to simply as a black pudding, pot pudding, or pudding meat. The most common word, however, was *Panhas* or some English equivalent like *ponhoss* or *pawnhoss*. These spellings and pronunciations moved out of Pennsylvania with English-speaking settlers during the eighteenth century and are still widely used in parts of the Piedmont South, western Maryland,

A selection of Panhas *labels showing the different dialect spellings of the word from Klingerstown and Hegins, Pennsylvania, and Harrisonburg, Virginia.*

the Valley of Virginia, and southern Ohio. Likewise, *Panhas* moved out of Germantown into the general language of the Pennsylvania Dutch, for most of them came from southwest Germany, where the word and dish are unknown. Thus both *scrapple* and *Panhas* are words and culinary concepts that have undergone a transfer from a very small group into the wider American culture. The evolution of the term *scrapple* is taken up in the next chapter; it is a story with many fascinating twists and turns, yet it too traces to Crefelder dialect.

The oldest known Westphalian recipes for *Panhas* do not date from the Middle Ages. The word and comments about the dish appeared with some frequency during the 1500s and became common by the late 1600s, especially in archival documents like tax returns (where food was paid in lieu of cash), estate records, and household accounts. Detailed *Panhas* recipes did not appear in cookbooks until the nineteenth century, when the whole process of making *Panhas* underwent adjustment to kitchen technology, most notably to the cookstove. Until that time, *Panhas* was really the domain of the country butcher, whose techniques, procedures, and recipes were part of an oral rather than a written tradition. The same could be said of scrapple making in colonial America.

While many home-style recipes for *Panhas* date from the early 1900s (like the recipe on page 92), the most widely circulated recipe for a professional butcher's version of *Panhas* is older. It appeared in

Weber's *Universal-Lexikon der Kochkunst* (Universal Lexicon of Cookery), which was published in the late 1800s. By that time, *Panhas* had become identified as an icon food of both Westphalian and Lower Rhineland cookery throughout German-speaking Europe; thus it was necessary to include it in this two-volume compendium. The recipe, however, was not a countrified version, but a rather sophisticated reinvention of the dish using beef and fancy meat stock and not a drop of pork blood. It was the Victorian-period equivalent of the new-wave scrapples discussed on page 74, and no doubt the whole concept was influenced by the German cookbook author Henrietta Davidis, who launched *Panhas* from the barnyard kettle into the well-appointed kitchens of middle-class Germany.

The final comments in the Weber recipe are perhaps the most significant, because they allude to a major change in meat consumption that occurred in post-1870s industrialized Germany. Formerly, pork butchering took place only in the fall or again in late January, several

Westphalian Panhas
(Professional Butcher's Version with Beef)

Boil until very tender 2 pounds (1 kg) of somewhat fatty boneless beef or 1 pound (500 g) of lean beef and 1 pound (500 g) of fatty pork in 1 gallon (4 liters) of water, together with an onion, some root vegetables, and salt. Remove the meat from the stock and cut away any skin and gristle. Dice the meat, then chop it as fine as possible. Strain the stock, which should measure about 3 to 3¹/₂ quarts (3 to 3¹/₂ liters) after cooking. Add the finely chopped meat to this, season with salt, ground pepper, cloves, and allspice. Bring the mixture to a boil, and sift in 1 pound (500 g) of buckwheat flour, so that after a good half hour of continuous stirring, the porridge becomes stiff and draws away from the kettle. Then pour it into earthenware dishes or bowls and store uncovered in a cool, airy place. The *Panhas* will keep 8 days during the summer and 14 days during the winter. It should be cut into ¹/₂-inch (1-cm) thick slices as required, and quickly fried on both sides in hot butter. Serve with potato dishes or with applesauce.

Translated from Johann Jakob Weber, ed., *Universal-Lexikon der Kochkunst* (Leipzig, 1897), vol. 2, p. 220. Measurements have been adapted to U.S. standards.

Westphalian Panhas
(Professional Butcher's Version with Pork Blood)

2 pig heads
1^1/$_2$ pounds (3 kilos) lean fresh pork belly
2 pounds (1 kilo) fatty bacon
fresh pork liver
fresh pork blood
salt and pepper
nutmeg, cloves, and marjoram
2 to 4 pounds (1 to 2 kilos) buckwheat flour

Cook the pig heads until tender, then remove the bones. Poach the pork belly until it is hot all the way through. Combine this with the bacon, liver, and the meat from the pig heads, and run it through a meat grinder adjusted to the coarsest setting.

Bring the cooking stock to a boil, then add the blood and ground meat. Let this cook for a short time, skim off the foam, and season to taste with salt, pepper, nutmeg, cloves, and marjoram. Lastly, bind the mixture with the buckwheat flour. Done!

Recipe of Erich Gundel, butcher in Wegberg-Beeck, Germany, 1991. Translation by William Woys Weaver.

---

weeks before the beginning of Lent. *Panhas* was not something people consumed in the summer. Yet the Weber recipe is clear that the dish could be kept for a week during hot weather. This comment was not addressed to the wives of farmers, but to professional butchers who now offered the dish all year round. This was possible because the meat-packing industry in Germany now produced fresh meat twelve months a year. Likewise, the well-off burgher's wife could purchase any of the required ingredients and make the dish herself at the whim of the moment.

Westphalian *Panhas* has undergone a large revival along with renewed interest in folk culture and regional cookery in Germany, especially since the 1970s. It now appears in every cookbook claiming to represent the culinary roots of the Lower Rhineland. This revival has also marked a shift in the way professional cooks handle the recipe, with a return to authenticity as one of the guiding themes. Authenticity is a highly subjective concept, just as "traditional" is an invention of the postindustrial milieu. Whatever the case, the recipe handed me in 1991 by Erich Gundel, a butcher in Wegberg-Beeck, represents the most recent phase in the *Panhas* story. I do not expect anyone to cook it, but anyone who does will readily notice that this recipe makes a very large batch of dark black scrapple. This may seem unappetizing to the American eye, but it is the type of scrapple that now appears in trendy restaurants specializing in local fare.

The quest for authenticity and tradition has been a long, ongoing process in German food history, and while much was written about foodways before the last war, an impressive quantity of material has been collected on Westphalian *Panhas* since 1945. The Institute for Popular Culture (Institut für Volkskunde) at the Wilhelm-Universität in Münster, Germany, has accumulated a large archive on this subject, especially in response to questionnaires sent out to older residents in the countryside. One such response, collected in 1958 and published by Karl Schmidthaus in 1964, touches on most of the major cultural aspects surrounding *Panhas* production.[10] The respondent pointed out that the white stock was sometimes drunk as a hot beverage, especially when butchering took place on a cold day—an ancient custom already described. The broth was also eaten as soup over a slice of bread. This was especially the case for invalids and children. And aside from being converted into *Panhas,* some of the thickened stock was used for making blood pancakes.

Blood pancakes *(Blutkuchen)* were at one time an important side dish associated with the butchering-day meal. In fact, German linguist Georg Andreas Bachem has attempted to link this ritual dish with the Celto-Roman origin of *Panhas.*[11] It was common practice during the Middle Ages to take the warm, foaming blood of the freshly killed pig, mix this with meal, and immediately cook the stiff batter on a portable griddle. Many butchering scenes, especially in German and Dutch art, show the blood being collected for this purpose.

In the region around Dortmund, *Panhas* finds its counterpart in *Potthas,* a term that in local dialect is generally understood to mean crock sausage or pot pudding. It is also a food gift consisting of a dish of fresh *Panhas,* a sampling of each sort of sausage made that day, and a piece of fresh pork. This food was distributed to the people who helped with the butchering; they in turn were expected to send a *Potthas* back when the host was asked to help them with their own butchering. In Pennsylvania, this food gift was commonly called a *Metzelsupp* (butcher's stew), after Palatine custom, but the word *Potthas* was preserved in some Pennsylvania Dutch families and recorded here and there in the nineteenth century. The origin of the term *Potthas* is still under debate. It derives either from the Vulgar Latin *pottus* or, more likely, from the Gaulish *potta;* both words mean a drink or beverage. The idea of sending around draughts of thick cooking stock to the participants in butchering-day activities is one further link to ancient custom.

Interestingly enough, this term has been preserved in yet another sense in the region around Münster, Germany, where it appears in connection with a local dish of medieval origin known as *Pfefferpotthas*. The name implies that it is more than just *Potthas*. Unfortunately, it is often mistranslated into English as "pepperpot," which only leads to confusion. Today, Münster *Pfefferpotthas* has evolved into a slightly sour meat stew thickened with fine white breadcrumbs. In the Middle Ages, it was a *Metzelsupp* thickened with gingerbread *(Pfefferkuchen)*, an indication that this is not really a food of peasant origin. Two versions of the dish appeared in *Das Kochbuch aus dem Münsterland* (Cookbook from the Münster Region), one of them submitted by Pinkus Müller, a popular restaurant in Münster.[12] Even though the publication of this cookbook was encouraged by the well-known European ethnographer Günter Wiegelmann, all the regional recipes have undergone a facelift to make them palatable to the widest readership possible. Lowly *Panhas* is nowhere mentioned.

Farther south, in the Hunsrück, the idea of eating the *Metzelsupp* as porridge disappeared at least a century earlier. This may have been due both to less poverty and to contact with French culinary ideas flowing over the border from the west during the eighteenth century. The basic structure of butchering day was the same, with a local butcher and a few neighbors coming to the farm to assist in the slaughtering, but all the dialect terminologies changed.[13] The plain white stock was called *Worschtsupp* (sausage soup), and it was served as the main midday meal for several days following the butchering session. Rather than thicken it the old way to a gruel consistency with oatmeal or buckwheat flour, it was common practice to chop or crumble dry bread rolls or to shred pancakes into the soup. A few slices of sausage were sometimes added. Furthermore, in this region, the gift of sausages and meat was called the *Prob,* from *Probe* (a test or tasting), rather than a *Metzelsupp* or *Pottas.*

It would be possible to move around the map of northern Germany and explore the innumerable local variations on the *Panhas* theme. According to the *Rheinisches Wörterbuch* (Dictionary of Lower Rhineland German), *Panhas* and its close relatives are known by quite a large number of synonyms, among them *Balkenbrei, Bünnick, Dätsch, Klappertüt, Klümpes, Knabbedapp, Krümpels, Krüpit, Prinz, Puttes,* and *Tuët,* to name just a few. Likewise, *Metzelsupp,* both as a soup and as a food gift, is still widespread in the Palatinate, and even across the Rhine in Baden-Württemberg, where the broth is often thickened with *Riwwle* (grated bits of dough) rather than with meal or flour. Since references to putting bread into the *Metzelsupp* appeared as early as 1448, it is fairly safe to presume that all of these varying food customs were common in medieval peasant culture during the butchering season, or *Schlachtmonat* (butchering month), as November was formerly called.

One of the main differences between the north German and more southern versions of *Panhas* was in the use of buckwheat flour. For many centuries, buckwheat has played an important role as a thickening agent in traditional north German and Holland Dutch scrapples. This has not always been the case, because the wild progenitor of buckwheat (*Fagopyrum esculentum* subspecies *ancestrale*) comes from Yunnan province in China. Cultivated buckwheat gradually spread westward across Asia during the early Middle Ages and was not introduced as an agricultural crop into the Lower Rhineland until the late 1400s. The German plant historian Udelgard Körber-Grohne has pointed out that buckwheat was imported from the East as early as the 900s, because archeological remains dating from that time have been found in old Polish and German trading sites.[14] Furthermore, local cultivation in the Rhineland varied from one region to the next, with the earliest evidence coming from Holland in the 1300s. Buckwheat did not become common in the rural diet of the entire North Sea region until the early seventeenth century, and Körber-Grohne cited buckwheat *Panhas* as a case in point. The question is, what grain did buckwheat replace, and why?

The obvious choice would be barley or oats, both of which were well adapted to the brackish soils of this region and were employed as Celtic food crops long before the period of Germanic migration. Yet in looking at late-medieval recipes like the blood pudding from Limburg on page 15, it is evident that the dark flour involved in butchering dishes must have been rye. There were probably several reasons for the shift from rye- to buckwheat-based porridges. Certainly one of them was the growth of distilleries in the 1600s, which allowed farmers to sell their rye quite profitably for *Karnbrantwein,* as rye whiskey was known. Rye was also further rectified for making finer spirits like Holland gin. Indeed, in the Berg region of the Rhineland, nearly every farmhouse possessed a gin still by 1700.[15] Also, when the hull was removed from the buckwheat seed, it could be milled to produce a perfectly white flour, much whiter than wheat. For a peasantry whose food was largely brown or some shade of gray, this whiteness gave buckwheat flour added status. But by removing the skin and hull, the nutritional value was greatly diminished.

Buckwheat had other recommendations, too, both as a green manure for intensive agriculture and as a fodder crop for hogs and dairy cattle. It is this last feature that evidently appealed most to the Holland Dutch. When they settled in New Netherlands in the 1640s and began populating the Hudson and Delaware River Valleys in America, they brought buckwheat with them. This was confirmed in 1775 by the author of *American Husbandry,* who pointed out that buckwheat was extensively grown in northern New Jersey and New York, and that it paid as well as wheat in terms of income.[16] This would imply that there was a large, established market for it already in place.

In Old Netherlands, buckwheat was planted on marshland recently cleared for farming. It was known to improve the soil in the polders. In America, it was an ideal first crop on "new ground," the term applied to freshly cleared fields. It gave the family milk cow something to eat, and it provided an easily harvested seed that could be converted to an inexpensive grade of flour with a few turns of a hand mill. To round out the economic equation, the waste chaff made excellent chicken and hog feed.

With so much buckwheat in their fields, it is not surprising that *Panhas* was common on the rural Dutch menu. But just as in Germany, the dish underwent name changes and slight alterations in the way it was made from one locality to the next. In Dutch Gelderland, German *Balkenbrei* became *balkenbrij, Panhas* became *pannharst,* and new expressions such as *pannevleesch* ("fry-meat") crept into the language. Some, like *schrapelkoekje*, had humorous double meanings (a surprise baby late in life), but others were quite descriptive.

The root word in *balkenbrij* is *balke* or *balge* (organ meat), which comes from *bake* or *buik*, an old Dutch term related to English bacon. While *balkenbrij* is the most commonly recorded word for scrapple in both the Netherlands and Belgium, the term is not recorded in any of the dialect word lists of so-called "Jersey Dutch," the colonial language of New Netherlands. It was a word used only in and around Holland, Michigan, settled by Hollanders in the nineteenth century.[17] The Dutch in colonial America used the term *beuling*, a general word for any sort of meat pudding, although strictly speaking it applied to meat puddings stuffed into skins, like the medieval blood pudding from Limburg. This takes us into a gray area, because the Dutch also put scrapple in sausage skins, and in fact, this type of *balkenbrij* is a legally recognized "indigenous" sausage in the Netherlands today.

Like the foodways, the Holland Dutch contribution to the buckwheat culture in colonial America has not been fully explored. On the other hand, there is copious reference to buckwheat in early American agricultural literature, even though food is not always the primary focus. Cultural geographer James Lemon, who has researched eighteenth-century farming patterns in the Delaware Valley, found clear statistical evidence that buckwheat was grown in small amounts in comparison with other grains on any one particular farm, but its cultivation was nevertheless widespread.[18] Since wheat was a cash crop in Pennsylvania and Maryland, the overall acreage devoted to buckwheat was much lower than in New Jersey and New York, yet this did not diminish its importance. Its role as an emergency food when wheat failed and as a source of flour for fall scrapple making are probably two important factors in these statistics. Because it could be grown on poorly cleared land, buckwheat was also a food favored by the rural poor, whose marginal lifestyle does not always surface in colonial records. This is confirmed by the eighteenth-century Lutheran minister Henry Melchior Muhlenberg, who was quick to observe that when the buckwheat failed, "it is hard for the poor."[19]

The German ethnographer Johann Noever has described the role of buckwheat as poverty food in its most unembellished simplicity.[20] In the Rhineland, the poor boiled buckwheat flour in water (or in milk,

Oak pot stick (mundle) for stirring scrapple from Sussex County, Delaware. This traditional shape, tracing to the Middle Ages, is one of the oldest forms found in early America. The mundle measures 14¹/₂ inches long and was found inside a fireplace boarded up about 1830.
ROUGHWOOD COLLECTION

if they were lucky enough to own a cow) and served it as gruel in a large common bowl. They called this dish *Dätsch,* in some localities a term also applied to scrapple. Each member of the family scooped out a hole in the mush and filled it with a dab of pork drippings or butter. They then mixed this with the gruel and ate from the spot directly in front of them. Hot scrapple "soup" was eaten the same way, and we know that the Pennsylvania Dutch often ate cornmeal mush in this manner, because references to such poverty meals survive from the early 1800s.

Job Roberts, in *The Pennsylvania Farmer,* noted that buckwheat made a nutritious flour, improved the soil, and was an excellent source of flowers for beekeepers, but said nothing about scrapple, living as he did in the heart of scrapple country.[21] Likewise, William Drown's *Farmer's Guide* recognized the merits of buckwheat as fodder and for beekeeping, yet he did note that it made an "agreeable bread."[22] By that he meant breadstuff, as it was more properly called—buckwheat cakes eaten warm from the griddle. Drown was a New Englander, so he could hardly be expected to know the particulars of scrapple making. But what he did share with Roberts and most of the other English-speaking population of colonial America was the knowledge of one colloquial word that stands at the center of this culinary story—the old English word *scrapple*. Furthermore, its Dutch cognate *schrapel* has the very same meaning. In a twist of dialect speech all too common in hearth talk, the names of utensils rubbed off on the foods made with them.

American Scrapple
and How It Got Its Name

"*The real American hog* is what is termed the wood hog; they are long in the leg, narrow on the back, short in the body, flat on the sides, with a long snout, very rough in their hair, in make more like the fish called a perch than anything I can describe." This frank assessment of our common rural pigs was made by Englishman Richard Parkinson in 1805.[23] It was this wily, foul-tempered beast, which could jump snake fences and destroy entire cornfields, that provided early America with its scrapple. The added importance of scrapple to country folk of that era is brought home when we consider what little meat was gotten off those old-style pigs. They were not bred for good characteristics; butchers just picked the fattest of the lot, and those that remained were used for increasing the stock. Some gentlemen farmers raised Chinese hogs, but the general run of porker was scrawny, lean, and even muscular. For those tough animals, scrapple was probably the best recipe for cooking it.

With the introduction of Chester Whites from England in the 1820s, hog breeding became more sophisticated. Likewise, the role of scrapple and its composition also changed. That is the same period when scrapple emerged from the shadows of history and appeared for the first time in American culinary literature. But lying behind this emergence was a two hundred-year evolution during which time both the dish and its many names came into being. Scrapple was the food of the common man, not the aristocrat; thus it is in the speech of the

A prize boar owned by Reuben Haines of Wyck, Germantown (Philadelphia), as depicted in an 1819 drawing. Its weight was 319 pounds, an indication of the small size of American pigs in the early nineteenth century. ROUGHWOOD COLLECTION

common man that we must look for clues about scrapple and how it acquired its name.

Unlike *Panhas,* which takes its name from an ancient cooking utensil, *scrapple* represents a fusion of several similar words that came together only during hog butchering. There is a lot of confusion among linguists who have attempted to trace the origin of the word, which is mentioned in English manuscript sources as early as 1397, and then connect it to scrapple the food. In the common speech of the Delaware Valley from the seventeenth century down to the nineteenth, there was more than one scrapple, yet there was only one word in English to express them all. In kitchen parlance, a scrapple was an ash rake or a dough scrapper, the same tool used for scrapping pork skins when making sausage; it was also any sort of leftover food—but not specifically "scraps." In garden parlance, it was a grubbing hoe. The word survives in the phrase hard to scrapple land or "hardscrabble"—too rocky to hoe.

In the Dutch and Low German-speaking communities of New Castle, Delaware; Germantown, Pennsylvania; and what is now Whitemarsh Township, northwest of Philadelphia, *schrapel* was also a grubbing hoe, and thus by extension, a *schrapelkoekje* (scrapple cake) was a hoecake. In the primitive conditions of the early settlers' cabins, the wide, rectangular blade of a grubbing hoe was often used as a makeshift griddle. This practice, as well as the term *hoecake*, persisted in the South much longer than in the North. John Hart, who was born in Kentucky in 1850, described his mother's pioneer kitchen in Parker County, Texas, during the 1860s this way: "The cooking utensils consisted of a three-legged skillet, oven [Dutch oven], dinner pot, tea kettle, a big iron shovel and a pair of pot hooks."[24] The big iron shovel served the same purpose as the old-time grubbing hoe: It was used as a hand-held griddle.

The word *scrapple* does have a counterpart in medieval Latin: *scrapul* or *scrupul* (sing.), and *scrapullus* (plural). This word derives from *scrapulatio* or *scapulatio* and appears as early as 1282 in medieval documents. However, the meaning is somewhat limited, since it applies to the trimmings or chips from dressed stone or wood. In common Middle English, "to scrapple" a log was to turn it into a dressed piece of timber, something house carpenters did in the New World when they squared off logs for log houses or made timbers for barns and finer dwellings.

This does not have a direct connection with food preparation, although it is well documented in England, Holland, and Germany that masons and roof tile makers often worked as butchers during the winter when they could not practice their main trade. This seasonal contact opens the possibility of a crossover point where the jargon of one profession entered the speech of a broader segment of society. That kind of exchange is not common, and to date, linguistic research has not uncovered evidence of such a word transition. The Dutch verb *scrappen* (to rasp) appears in numerous Dutch manu-

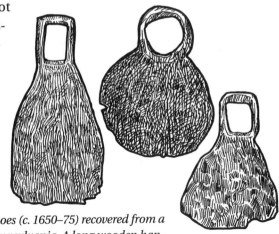

Colonial scrapples or grubbing hoes (c. 1650–75) recovered from a Susquehannock burial site in Pennsylvania. A long wooden handle fit through the hole at the top of each blade. PENNSYLVANIA HISTORICAL AND MUSEUM COMMISSION

script cookery books dating from the Middle Ages, and by extension, culinary *scrapplings* were the raspings created by grating bread or cheese. If scrapple were made with breadcrumbs, this avenue of origin would seem convincing. It is not the shredding or the mincing of the meat that gave scrapple its name, even though this is the most widely accepted explanation. The preexistence of terms for scrapple in medieval Latin and Middle English invalidates its narrow definition as a diminutive of *scrap,* an explanation put forth in Mitford Mathews's *Dictionary of Americanisms* and quoted so many times that it is accepted as fact. The explanation sounds logical, but it is not even close to the mark. The word is derived from Crefelder dialect, and German ethnographer Paul Sartori noted this in the 1920s.[25] The root word is *Kröp* (a slice), and especially the diminutive form *Kröppel.* Thus, *Panhaskröppel* means simply a slice of *Panhas.* The *skröppel* became *scrapple* because it sounded like a word English speakers knew already. In this way, *scrapple* evolved from the name of a slice of pot pudding to the name of the naturalized dish itself. But the use of this term in this particular way was limited to Philadelphia and its immediate environs for almost two hundred years.

In Ernst Meier's 1915 survey of Ravensburg butchering expressions, it is clear that the most common forms of *Panhas* were made with the haslet (heart, liver, and lungs attached as one piece) and other internal organs, and that clove was an essential spice.[26] These ingredients are implied in the Friesian scrapple called *Kröse* (from *Gekröse,* meaning organ meat), made with pearl barley and mentioned in local records as early as 1574. This was not a hard and fast rule, however, because other parts of the pig were also frequently employed. They included the feet, ears, tail, and snout, although separately each of these items was considered a worthy subject for specialized recipes. The feet could be used for making souse, the ears could be cut into strips and cooked like pasta, and the snouts could be pickled. Furthermore, many surviving recipes for German *Panhas* also mention the addition of onions, bay leaves, and generous quantities of black pepper. It is interesting that old-style Philadelphia scrapple rarely included onions, while onions were almost universally called for in the South, even in liver mush and liver pudding. And in a departure from most of the Old World recipes, Philadelphia scrapple also employed sage, savory, and perhaps even marjoram. These were herbs that Anglo-Americans put into puddings intended as stuffings.

One of the earliest and most unambiguous references to Philadelphia scrapple appears in the 1830s diary of Rebecca Rhoads, a Quaker who lived for a while on Green Street in what was then the northern fringe of Philadelphia. As brief as it is, her comment has provided some useful insights into how scrapple was made in urban households during that period, especially when other bits of information in the diary are pieced together. Her husband's cousin Ezekiel Rhoads was an important player. He owned a farm at Norriton near Norristown, Pennsylvania, and worked as a produce broker who brought food and livestock down Germantown Pike into the city once a week. He and his wife normally stayed overnight at Rebecca's house during those trips.

Cousin Ezekiel was the source for the bulk of Rebecca's groceries, including a large hog that he brought to her house at 3 Green Street on December 28, 1832.[27] He helped cut up the animal in her backyard while Rebecca and other members of her household salted the meat they needed for the coming year. The next day, Rebecca noted in her diary that she "made sassage & ponhors puddings with the poark; finished about three o'clock." Her spelling was never the best, an indication that she was doubtless a plain country girl, especially since she prepared a number of rural dishes, like rabbit pot pie, which cannot be found in period cookbooks. At least she was consistent, throughout her twenty years of diary keeping, in writing *Panhas* as *ponhors*. She never once used the word *scrapple,* but her purchases of buckwheat flour a week or so in advance of butchering (always in late December) were clear evidence that she was thinking ahead and planning her recipe. Her actual working recipe has not been preserved.

Two points are worth noting: Even though she was living in a thoroughly Quaker neighborhood of the city, Rebecca Rhoads used a *Pennsylfaanisch* term for scrapple. This may not seem unusual if we take into account that most of the hog butchers in the city were Germans who would have called it *Panhas.*[28] One of the best-known hog butchers in Philadelphia at that time was Christian H. Laudenslager, who did not live too far from the Rhoads residence. His wife leased a stall in the Camptown Market above Brown Street, where she presumably sold fresh pork, sausage, and scrapple by the pan.[29]

Regardless of the source of her terminology for scrapple, Rebecca Rhoads recognized it as a type of pudding and even called it that consistently throughout her life. She had no cultural awareness that scrapple evolved out of a gruel or soup; it was just a frugal way to use up leftovers. On the other hand, Rhoads's *Panhas* may serve as an example from the halfway point in the gradual process of acculturation that was taking place between the Pennsylvania Dutch and English-speaking communities. Scrapple was a minority term in the 1830s, but within fifty years, it became the dominant word for the dish. The basic recipe also underwent changes in this cross-cultural process. These changes may be traced through cookbooks.

What the Cookbooks Say

Since scrapple is such an important food in the Pennsylvania Dutch diet, the most logical place to look for a recipe would be in a cookbook from that culture. Unfortunately, most published recipes are of very recent vintage. The oldest published Pennsylvania Dutch recipe collection was compiled about 1846–47 by Harrisburg printer Gustav Peters and printed posthumously in 1848 under the title *Die Geschickte Hausfrau* (The Handy Housewife).[30] Peters's pocket-size cookbook became extremely popular, remaining in print into the 1880s. Although the recipes were written in Pennsylvania High German and adapted to peculiarly *Pennsylfaanisch* taste preferences, the range of dishes represented old-fashioned middle-class American cookery of the period. There was no recipe for scrapple, no recipe for sauerkraut, not even a pot pie. It took the cultural shock of the Civil War to show the Pennsylvania Dutch just how distinctive they were, thus heralding in a cultural renaissance that found expression in such rustic identity foods as Centennial cake (now known as shoofly pie), chow-chow, and chicken corn soup.

On the European side of the Atlantic, there are a number of pamphlet-size German cookbooks comparable to *Die Geschickte Hausfrau* in format, content, and period of publication. *Die bürgerliche Küche* (The Middle Class Kitchen), printed at Uhrfahr-Linz in Austria about 1851, was sold as a series, each volume or number of which was devoted to a specific culinary topic and could stand alone as a complete work. The first volume was devoted to meat dishes. Like *Die Geschickte Hausfrau,* this cookbook did not contain recipes that at that time were considered rustic or peasant. There was nothing even vaguely related to meat gruels, and very little pork. Nearly all of the recipes dealt with luxury meats like veal or lamb, or in some cases beef, prepared as cutlets, roulades, or elaborate roasts with relevant sauces.

Regardless of the cheap quality of the cookbook, this was the cookery of an aspiring rural middle class. Ironically, many of these same recipes are today treated as "traditional" in Austria and South Germany.

Cookbooks did not become a forum for truly rustic fare until industrialization created a large gap between urban and rural lifestyles in the latter part of the nineteenth century. This, together with evolving concepts of national identity, gave rise to nostalgia for the simple ways of rural life and a romanticizing of peasant culture and foods. Scrapple eventually found its way into cookbooks once there was a general recognition that it had become an identity food, both locally and nationally. In Philadelphia, this connection was completed by Quaker writers, presumably because they saw scrapple as a symbol (like cream cheese) of Quaker farming and a food that linked them to other plain religious sects in the region.

Recipes for scrapple are useful only to people who have not grown up on a farm where they would have seen it made firsthand, and to those living outside the geographic area where the dish is a familiar occurrence. Thus scrapple became good material for agricultural journals, which extolled certain regional foods for their frugality, economy, and good taste. Most of the earliest scrapple recipes can be traced to such agricultural publications. This should not be surprising, given the fact that scrapple production was generally a male task on butchering day. If the first shift that took place in the evolution of American scrapple was the shift to widespread use of cornmeal, the second shift was the move from oral tradition to written recipe—from word of mouth among farmers and butchers to the printed word for kitchen cooks. In the process of creating a written recipe for stovetop cookery, the choice of ingredients underwent gradual changes. This occurred in tandem with changing attitudes about pork, especially about those parts of the animal deemed most fit for the middle-class table.

The first Philadelphia cookbook to publish a scrapple recipe was Hannah Bouvier Peterson's *National Cook Book,* which first appeared in 1850. Her recipe is reproduced in the accompanying sidebar. Her directions are well detailed, and it is evident that she had adapted her procedure to stovetop cookery. She also preferred to use cornmeal alone, and probably small white hominy in the style of southern scrapples. Her comment about the denseness of buckwheat is quite valid, because if it is not cooked thick enough, it will make the scrapple runny when it is fried in the pan.

Scrapple (Philadelphia)

This is generally made of the head, feet, and any pieces which may be left after having made sausage meat.

Scrape and wash well all the pieces designed for the scrapple, put them in a pot with just as much water as will cover them. Add a little salt, and let them boil slowly till the flesh is perfectly soft, and the bones loose. Take all the meat out of the pot, pick out the bones, cut it up fine, and return it to the liquor in the pot. Season it with pepper, salt, and rubbed sage, to the taste. Set the pot over the fire, and just before it begins to boil, stir in gradually as much Indian meal as will make it as thick as mush. Let it boil a few minutes, take it off, and pour it in pans. When cold, cut it in slices, flour it, and fry it in hot lard, or sausage fat.

Some prefer buckwheat meal; this is added in the same manner as the Indian. Indian meal is preferable, as it is not so solid as buckwheat.

Sweet marjoram may be added with the sage, if preferred.

From Hannah Bouvier Peterson, *The National Cook Book* (1855), 57.

Aunt Mary's *Philadelphia Housewife* was the next to publish a scrapple recipe and use that name for the dish.[31] But her recipe lacked many vital details (it did not even mention the word *meat*), did not list the herbs and spices (aside from salt and pepper), gave no proportions, and used only cornmeal as a thickener. Since it was essentially a type of cornmeal-mush-with-meat of a type similar to Peterson's scrapple and the Mennonite Ham Scrapple recipe on page 89, it was much more like the liver mush scrapples popular in the Upper South. Scrapples of this southern type were also popular in South Jersey, Lower Delaware, and Eastern Shore Maryland.

Aunt Mary's scrapple recipe was not the only recipe to appear in print in 1855. Evidently, a request for a scrapple recipe was published in the *Rural New Yorker* in 1854, and this was answered in the February 10, 1855, issue with a scrapple recipe of considerable originality. It does not appear anywhere else in cookbooks and must be an old family recipe, as its contributor claimed, dating to somewhere around 1800. It came from Wellsboro, Pennsylvania, and it is interesting that the *Rural New Yorker* put the word *scrapple* in quotes, treating it like a colloquialism as opposed to a well-known word. The recipe is worth repeating because it contains several points not found in others of this period. It is reproduced below.

This recipe runs against the general pattern in that it employs head meat slightly flavored (if at all) with liver. The presence of two or three hog jowls would seem to suggest that the butchering of several pigs had taken place and that something else had been done with the other livers, haslets, and sundry meats. Indeed, three hog jowls and a liver could pass for the butcher's portion, part of what was normally paid to a journeyman butcher for his day's work. One thing for certain—the Wellsboro correspondent was not a Quaker, or she would have dated her recipe differently.

While by no means the oldest, the Philadelphia scrapple recipe that best preserved the oral traditions of an eighteenth-century urban butcher was the recipe (page 36) published by Quaker cookbook author Elizabeth Nicholson. It appeared in her *Economical Cook and House-Book.*

The structure of her recipe, and especially the use of the archaic term *haslet,* would point to an interview with an old-time country butcher, perhaps a member of the Society of Friends to which she

"Scrapple"

I observe a call for a recipe for making "Scrapple" and some other homely dishes. Here is one that has been a favorite, with two generations.

Boil two or three pig's "faces," a liver, chine-bones, etc. (or omit the liver, if you choose), till the meat comes off the bones and will pick to pieces readily. Take out the meat, and half thicken the liquid with Indian meal, which allow to boil, whilst you pick the meat off the bones, and chop the liver fine; then return the meat, etc., into the pot, and stir in buckwheat flour, till it is thick as thick mush. This done, season the mixture with pepper, salt, and powdered sage, and put it into pans to cool. Next morning, fry it brown in slices, and see if your children will not decide that the "waste is the best after all." E. Wellsboro, Pa., Feb. 5, 1855.

From *Rural New Yorker,* February 10, 1855. *Note:* By "pig's faces," the author of this recipe means hog jowls, the head cleaned of eyes, brain, and snout. The "chine" was a cut along the spine; it is called the *Rickmeesel* in *Pennsylfaanisch.*

Scrapple (Philadelphia)

Take a pig's haslet and as much offal lean and fat pork as you wish, to make scrapple; boil them well together in a small quantity of water until they are tender; chop them fine, after taking them out of the liquor; season, as sausage: then skim off the fat that has arisen where the meat was boiled, to make all soft, throw away the rest of water, and put this altogether in the pot; thickening it with 1/2 buckwheat and 1/2 Indian. Let it boil up, then pour out in pans to cool. Slice and fry it in sausage-fat, after the sausage is done.

From Elizabeth Nicholson, *Economical Cook and House-Book* (Philadelphia, 1857), 18.

belonged. This is a justifiable assumption, since it was the object of her cookbook to support Quaker-owned businesses that favored the abolition of slavery. Many of those businesses are mentioned by name throughout the text. For example, under meat choppers and sausage stuffers, Nicholson recommended Paschall Morris & Company at 7th and Market Streets, Philadelphia—a possible source for her scrapple recipe. Morris sold agricultural supplies as well as a large inventory of seeds from his warehouse, not to mention Nicholson's cookbook. Other old butchering terms that appear elsewhere in her recipes, such as "pelted calf's head," meaning an unskinned head, provide further evidence of Nicholson's contact with someone familiar with technical words not used in common speech. Whatever her source, Nicholson was careful to place scrapple in a very specific category of foods known in Philadelphia as "breakfast relishes." These were savory foods, as opposed to sweet dishes, and included such items as beefsteaks, sausage patties, souse, head cheese, and broiled or baked tomatoes.

Four key elements in Nicholson's recipe are worth noting. The first is the reference to the haslet and offal as ingredients. The haslet was a specific piece or cut of the animal, commonly consisting of the heart, lights (lungs), and liver, all loosely connected in one piece. It could be purchased from butchers and is depicted in the accompanying woodcut. Offal refers to other internal organs.

According to Thomas DeVoe's *Market Assistant*, haslets were seldom seen in most East Coast markets by the 1860s because they were generally put into meat puddings, a practice consistent with urban scrapple making at that time.[32] His observation also confirms that a shift had taken place in urban American cookery: Haslets by themselves had fallen out of fashion save in exceptional cases. Festive recipes for Christmas or New Year are an excellent case in point. One such holdover recipe appeared in an 1856 cookbook by Quaker confectioner Hannah Widdifield, in the form of haslet sauce for roast suckling pig.[33] This archaic and nostalgic dish could have come right out of the 1600s.

Elsewhere in the Middle States, in small culture pockets where very traditional food habits persisted, haslet cookery retained an important place in the diet well into the late 1800s, although as a special occasion food. In eastern North Carolina, one of the few places in that state where the term was used, the haslet was a standard gift food to neighbors during hog butchering. Tidewater Virginia and South Jersey were two other areas where haslet cookery persisted. One of the most interesting of all the regional haslet dishes preserved from the nineteenth century is a recipe for pork haslet and liver prepared as a "made dish" in the style of chafing dish cookery. The recipe (page 38) comes from a Camden, New Jersey, cookbook. The term "made dish" harks back to eighteenth-century American cooking terminology, as though this were a platter of pork dainties set out at a "high meal" where a freshly killed suckling pig might be served. In style, with the hard-cooked eggs, dash of cayenne pepper, and "some wine" (Madeira, to be sure), this reads like a 1790s Philadelphia side dish, and probably a caterer's recipe at that.

Prior to the 1830s, the haslet was quite often referred to as the *pluck* in everyday American speech. It was highly valued in the eighteenth and early nineteenth centuries, well worth cooking as a special dainty on butchering day. Since it was not considered waste meat, it would not have gone into country scrapple. Elizabeth Nicholson's recipe was predicated on

Woodcut showing the haslet. From an eighteenth-century cookbook. ROUGHWOOD COLLECTION

Haslet and Liver

Take a haslet and liver, boil until tender, chop up a portion of both, put in a pan with black and red pepper and salt and hard boiled eggs; cut up a large piece of butter; a little water and some wine; dredge in a little flour and let it boil up.

From *The Housekeeper's Help: A Collection of Valuable Recipes Contributed by The Ladies of St. Paul's P.E. Church* (Camden, NJ, 1886), 19. *Note:* By "a portion of both," the author of this recipe is saying that the larger part of what has been boiled is to be used for something else, most likely scrapple.

the fact that there had been a change in taste concerning the haslet. In fact, she addressed her recipe to people who did not live on farms. Her meat ingredients needed to be purchased from a butcher, since a haslet and offal had to be boiled to create the white stock basic to her scrapple recipe. On a farm where butchering and sausage making had occurred, there would have been a large kettle of white stock already on hand; no need to cook a haslet. The only necessary step would be to thicken the broth.

The second feature of Nicholson's recipe (in the order mentioned) is the seasonings, which she noted should be the same as for sausage. Her recipe for sausage precedes the scrapple recipe and is seasoned with salt, pepper, ground cloves, and sage. Medieval and even more recent Old World scrapples included a great many seasonings, largely due to ideas about achieving a balance in the perceived healthfulness of the dish, as well as the perceived preservative benefits of certain herbs. Both sage and savory, for example, contain antimicrobial constituents.

The third feature of Nicholson's recipe is also one of the most significant: skimming off the fat. None of the ingredients she called for were fatty, although she did allow for some fatty meat. In any case, the fat was cooked out and removed, thus the mixture was relatively lean as processed meat products go, so lean in Nicholson's case that she recommended frying the scrapple in sausage drippings. Modern commercial scrapples need no added fat for frying because a large amount of fatty material is ground into the meat mix. This is an important departure from the old traditional scrapples, which were low-fat by definition.

The fourth and final point is the thickening. Nicholson's meat mixture resembles a soft batter or fine puree, thus her scrapple is much denser and meatier-tasting than most present-day commercial scrapples. She thickened this batter with equal parts of buckwheat flour and "Indian" cornmeal—not the gritty cornmeal used today for cornbread, but meal from stone-ground white flour corn similar to what is used in making tortillas. Flour corns were grown in many parts of the Middle States for use in cookery until the Civil War. Cheap, processed wheat flour more or less replaced this type of flour by the 1870s; only the flint corns used for mush persisted. Thus the primary historic differences between Philadelphia-style scrapple and Pennsylvania Dutch *Panhas* were in the different choices of cornmeal and waste meats.

The Philadelphia Quakers preferred white Menomonee flour corn prior to the Civil War, whereas the Pennsylvania Dutch preferred the same yellow cornmeal they used for cooking mush. Yellow cornmeal is now used in all of the commercial scrapples produced in Pennsylvania. In other parts of the country, especially the South, white cornmeal is the ingredient of choice. Fine white cornmeal is probably what was used in Elizabeth Ellicott Lea's recipe for scrapple (page 40), since her cookery was based on an essentially Chesapeake or rural Maryland tradition. Lea was a Quaker born in 1793 at Ellicott City, Maryland, where her father was in the milling business. She spent most of her life on a farm she inherited at Sandy Springs and died there in 1858. She is best remembered for her popular cookbook called *Domestic Cookery.*

Elizabeth Nicholson made numerous references to Lea in her cookbook, but she did not use Lea's scrapple recipe. Elizabeth Lea's *Domestic Cookery* was a long labor of love that first appeared in 1845. The scrapple recipe she published was tested at Sandy Springs, but she collected it in the 1820s, when she began compiling the recipe collection that evolved into *Domestic Cookery.* That manuscript was begun in 1821 at Brandywine Mills in Delaware, where Lea lived with her husband shortly after her marriage; it survives in the hands of Lea's descendants, who permitted me to see it in 1983.

The chronology of Elizabeth Lea's scrapple recipe is important because it is the oldest datable recipe for American scrapple and one of the first to adapt the dish to stovetop cookery. The intention of Lea's cookbook was to teach young brides how to cook from scratch, but the underlying premise was that her young brides were living on farms, therefore butchering was done at home. This is why her

Scrapple (Sandy Springs, Maryland)

Take eight pounds of scraps of pork, that will not do for sausage; boil it in four gallons of water; when tender, chop it fine, strain the liquor and pour it back into the pot; put in the meat; season it with sage, summer savory, salt and pepper to taste; stir in a quart of cornmeal; after simmering a few minutes, thicken it with buckwheat flour very thick; it requires very little cooking after it is thickened, but must be stirred constantly.

From Elizabeth Ellicott Lea, *Domestic Cookery* (1851), 171–72.

scrapple recipe begins with scraps of pork left over from sausage making. Lea also provides some useful advice about the process of home butchering:

> The pepper should be ground and ready some days before it is needed, as the pork season in the country is (while it lasts) one of the busiest in the year; everything should be prepared before hand that you possibly can. It is a good idea to plan to have plenty of bread and pies baked, and a quantity of apples stewed, vegetables washed and ready to cook, so that every member of the family, that is able, may devote herself to the work of putting away the meat which is of so much importance for the coming year.[34]

It is obvious from all of Lea's meat-preservation recipes that there are men somewhere in the background doing the actual killing and cutting up of the carcasses. It is the women who must know how to process the meat into sausages and other products like scrapple. It is also evident from her precautionary comment above that the traditional butchering day (in late November or early December) was capped by a large meal and that the meat for this meal came from the slaughtered animals. For the rural farmer in the Middle States, scrapple was no longer a simple porridge shared by the butchering participants; it had already evolved by the 1820s into a specific kind of winter breakfast food.

The rural character of Lea's recipe, as opposed to the citified version of Elizabeth Nicholson's, is evident in the coarser texture, the choice of cornmeal, less meat, and her use of readily available herbs (sage and summer savory) rather than spices like cloves or nutmeg. In this regard, Lea's recipe closely resembles the *Panhas* of the Pennsylvania

Dutch and provides some explanation for why authors in the nine-teenth century made a distinction between Philadelphia scrapple and the rural sorts. Among the Pennsylvania Dutch, scrapple retained a dual character for a much longer period than among their English-speaking neighbors. For the Pennsylvania Dutch, it was both a gruel and a fried breakfast dish; for the Anglo-Americans, it was an accul-turated food prepared specifically as a "breakfast relish." The excep-tion to this rule was the poverty cookery of Appalachia and the Upper South, where scrapples were often eaten as hot pork mush.

A serious discussion about the differences between Quaker and Pennsylvania Dutch scrapple surfaced in an article on the Pennsylva-nia Dutch in the October 1869 issue of *Atlantic Monthly.* The author was Lancaster County Quaker Phebe Earle Gibbons (1821–93), who later included the piece in her 1872 book, *Pennsylvania Dutch and Other Essays.* Gibbons's firsthand descriptions of her Pennsylvania Dutch neighbors launched the beginning of a tourist industry focused on the Amish Mennonites, but it is her scrapple commentary that interests us here. After discussing the *Metzelsupp* and how it was often distributed to poor widows as well as to those who helped in the butchering work, Gibbons differentiated between liver pudding and scrapple or *Panhas:*

> *We* make scrapple from the skin, a part of the livers, and heads, with the addition of corn-meal; but instead, our "Dutch" neighbors make *liverwurst* ("woorsht"), or meat pudding, omitting the meal, and this compound, stuffed into the larger entrails, is very popular in Lancaster market. Some make *pawn-haus* from the liquor in which the pudding-meat was boiled, adding thereto corn-meal. The name is properly *pann-haas,* and signifies, perhaps, panned-rabbit. It is sometimes made of richer material.[35]

Gibbons italicized *we* in her comments because she was referring specifically to her own well-to-do Quaker household at Bird-in-Hand, where the Gibbons family lived. It is evident from her list of ingredients that the composition of Gibbons's scrapple was considerably richer than many other local recipes, since it consisted of meats normally set aside elsewhere in the United States for head cheese.[36] The fact that the heads and livers were treated as waste products may be interpreted as evidence of the type of cultural divide that existed at the time between more urban and educated households (like those of the Quakers) and the Pennsylvania Dutch. The livers were highly prized by the Dutch, but Gibbons's remark that liver puddings were popular in the Lancaster markets was also an allusion to the fact that these puddings were more often made for sale and not eaten by their makers. This was a common practice among frugal German peasants in Europe, who depended on urban markets as their only steady source of cash.

Liver puddings were put up in what were known as the "great skins," or the larger entrails, as Gibbons called them—the large intestines. These sausages were very large, indeed, about a foot long, and nothing like the dainty liverwurst sold in markets today. The fillings were coarse in texture, more like a meat and liver hash than a refined pâté. When the filling was poured into crocks, the name changed to pot pudding or pudding meat. In many rural households, this was served as breakfast or supper food. It was fried in a skillet until it fell apart, then poured over buckwheat cakes, sliced bread, or mush and eaten like gravy. Outside the Pennsylvania Dutch communities, this type of fried gravy was made with head cheese or, in the South, with liver mush.

Phebe Gibbons astutely noted that she had never seen head cheese among the Dutch, while it was fairly common in most American farm markets of the period. The reason for this is that among the Dutch, roasted or smoked-and-boiled pig's head was considered a great delicacy, just as it had been among the English in the seventeenth century. While Victorian Americans had begun discarding the practice of eating animal heads, the Dutch still held on to this old custom. It did not completely die out until the decline in home butchering toward the end of the nineteenth century. However, once the hog's head fell into the category of waste meat, it became a common additive in commercial scrapple, and it became an easy ingredient for recipe writers to recommend, since it was cheap.

It is clear that the makeup of scrapple has undergone considerable change over time, and that the various types and grades of mixtures have given rise to a great deal of confusion over the differences between scrapple, *Panhas,* and rural versus urban recipes. The only way to clarify this is to take a look at a working recipe used by a rural butcher and then compare it with one of the stovetop recipes already discussed—Elizabeth Lea's in particular. The butcher's recipe, given verbatim on the following page, comes from the Brunk family of Royersford, Pennsylvania.

First of all, this recipe was written down for the butcher's personal use, not for other eyes to read. This explains the casual lack of detail,

---

Scrapple

4 - 14 qt. buckets of broth and water
1 lard can of meat
15 tablespoons salt
7 tablespoons pepper, only 3¹/₂ Watkins pepper
flour to stiffen:
    1 part buckwheat
    2 parts flour
    3 parts cornmeal

Recipe of Paul Brunk, as published in the *Goschenhoppen Region* 1:3 (1969), 19.

---

yet it is typical of the sort of "outline recipe" that derives from oral tradition. The recruitment of buckets or some other readily available container to measure out ingredients is also typical of true folk cookery. For someone who lives on a farm and who makes scrapple every year, the recipe is detailed enough and probably not even necessary. But for the reader, I shall interpolate a few points so that the culinary picture is made even clearer.

The liquid part of the recipe works out to 14 gallons (56 liters). Brunk's lard can of meat is either a 10-pound (5 kg) or 25-pound (12¹/₂ kg) tin, more likely the latter. Nothing has been said about what part of the animal constituted the "meat," but we may be fairly certain that about 25 pounds (12¹/₂ kg) of meat was involved, based on the amount of liquid called for. In terms of the whole carcass, this is not much meat, not much more than a decent-size ham. It is doubtful that any of the head meat was used in this recipe, since there would be plenty enough from the bones.

The reference to using less of Watkins brand pepper than regular black pepper makes sense, taking into account that the Watkins mix contained red pepper, so it was hotter. The mix of buckwheat, wheat flour, and cornmeal should work out to about the same weight as the meat, because the meat and cereal parts of scrapple are generally equal. However, the quality of the flours may vary, so adjustments must be made. Prior to the Civil War, when spelt flour was often used in place of wheat flour, more of it was required because of the way it absorbs water. The most important point is that the Brunk recipe cannot be cooked on a stove; it must be managed outdoors or in a special shed for butchering. This is how scrapple was made before it underwent domestication for stovetop cookery, before it passed from a primarily outdoor male task to an indoor female activity.

Pre-stovetop scrapple was also treated differently, not necessarily as an end product, but as a multifunctional ingredient set aside to be converted into other foods. More than thirty years ago, Berks County butcher Newton Bachman provided valuable insights into this old practice.[37] According to Bachman, it was often customary to divide the freshly made scrapple into two large batches. One batch was put down in crocks filled three-fourths full, then sealed with lard. This could be kept in a cold cellar for several months, dipped out as required, and used as filling in half-moon pies and dumplings, or mixed with chopped bread and diced potatoes as stuffing in roasts. The other half of the scrapple was converted into mincemeat for pies. Chopped apple *Schnitz* (dried apples), dried pears, or other fruits were mixed into the scrapple, along with molasses and a generous quantity of rye whiskey. This type of scrapple could be kept in cool storage for several years. It was the basic Christmas pie for poor farmers all over the Middle States, and a popular breakfast food during the coldest months of the winter.

It is possible to find any number of old-style large-batch scrapple recipes in professional butchering manuals. *Secrets of Meat Curing and Sausage Making,* issued by B. Heller & Company of Chicago in 1908, was particularly effective in placing scrapple recipes in the hands of many small-town American butchers. This book has had a long-lasting effect, and the scrapple recipe is still in use by many small firms, including Mom Wilson's Country Sausage Mart in North Delaware, Ohio. On the other hand, scrapple was treated by the Hellers as a commercial, profit-generating product, not as a cultural phenomenon with an admittedly complex history. Interest in the cultural connotations of food is only of very recent date, and it was—much to her credit—Nancy Hasson Roan of the Goschenhoppen Historians in Vernfield, Pennsylvania, who rescued the Brunk recipe from oblivion.

Salt glaze scrapple crock, Philadelphia, c. 1840.
EX. MARY LARKIN THOMAS COLLECTION, PHOTO BY
WILLIAM WOYS WEAVER

The prosaic, countrified character of scrapple was one of the main reasons it was never dignified with the sort of literary interest devoted to other types of local foods during the early part of the nineteenth century; pepperpot is an excellent case in point. Philadelphia cookbook author Eliza Leslie avoided scrapple and anything else that seemed to her unfashionable. Not one of her books contains a recipe for scrapple; it was simply too "farmish" (a term she often employed for things she disdained) to fit into her scheme of refined behavior. This prejudice is rather odd in light of the fact that Leslie never hesitated to print recipes for bologna sausage, Westphalian ham, soused pig's feet, liver puddings, pepperpot, or wart remedies.

Consistent with this lack of literary interest, there is no mention of the dish in *Mackenzie's Five Thousand Receipts,* even though the 1830 book was Americanized by Leslie's contemporary, Philadelphia physician James Mease (1771–1846). This is all the more surprising as Mease took great care to single out other Philadelphia specialties, including Elizabeth Goodfellow's lemon pudding, the forerunner of lemon meringue pie. On the other hand, lemon pudding was considered genteel in 1830, whereas scrapple was not.

Scrapple did eventually arrive, socially speaking, once it became elevated to the realm of middle-class home cookery, but it was not Leslie who gave it that boost. In the 1867 *Mackenzie's Ten Thousand Receipts,* a book that the original Mackenzie hardly would have recognized, a recipe for scrapple appeared without comment. That recipe can be traced to Elizabeth Ellicott Lea's *Domestic Cookery,* and its inclusion may have been influenced by the fact that the publisher of the 1867 edition was T. Ellwood Zell, a well-known Quaker. Lea's recipe was repeated again in Henry Hartshorne's *Household Cyclopedia of General Information,* another Zell publication.[38] As a result, Elizabeth Lea's recipe became one of the most widely copied and disseminated of all the nineteenth-century scrapple recipes. Only Sarah Tyson Rorer's scrapple recipe, introduced at the Columbian Exposition in Chicago in 1893, received greater circulation.

The most effective booster for scrapple occurred in 1876, with the opening of the United States Centennial Exposition in Philadelphia. The exposition brought thousands of visitors to the city, who were able to sample scrapple in local hotels and in food concessions on the fairgrounds. The Centennial Exposition also heralded a surge of interest in historic sites and a nostalgic fascination with colonial cookery, thus foods like scrapple, pepperpot, and terrapin were showcased as local old-time specialties. Ella Myers's 1876 *Centennial Cook Book and General Guide,* which was both a cookbook and an illustrated guide to local historic sites, not only featured recipes for such regional Philadelphia dishes as pepperpot and sauerkraut, but also included one of the earliest printed recipes for southern-style liver mush. This surge of patriotic boosterism had a lasting effect on national cookbook writing, because after 1876, scrapple began to appear regularly in cookbooks claiming to reflect authentic American cookery. This trend became even more pronounced as the century progressed, because like so many other regional foods, scrapple set Americans apart from the great wave of immigrants who were streaming into the country at that time, especially from Eastern and Southern Europe. In many respects, scrapple became a red-white-and-blue icon food, and it has remained that way ever since.

Samuel Stehman Haldeman (1812–80), scion of yet another old Lancaster County family and a professor at the University of Pennsylvania, was one of the first individuals to attempt a scholarly definition of scrapple. It appeared in his book on linguistics called *Pennsylvania Dutch: A Dialect of South German with an Infusion of English.* Haldeman described scrapple as "maize flour boiled in the metzel-soup, afterwards fried and seasoned like hare."[39] "Maize flour," or flour corn, harks back to the Quaker recipe of Elizabeth Nicholson, and Haldeman recognized that the white stock was in fact the *Metzelsupp* in its most primitive, medieval form: the basis for a porridge still served at that time in some Pennsylvania Dutch communities, as well as the gift of meat given out at butchering. Where he and many others stumbled was in the folk etymology of *Panhas,* misreading the second half of the word as *Hase,* German for hare—perhaps taking a journalistic cue from Phebe Earle Gibbons, who was herself fluent in German.

This confusion was fortified to some extent by the tendency in southeastern Pennsylvania English speech to pronounce Welsh rarebit as Welsh rabbit, thus mistakenly connecting hares and rabbits with faux foods fried or baked in skillets. In actuality, the proper *Pennsylfaanisch* term for such foods is *blind,* as in *blinde Hase* ("blind rabbit") or *blinde Fische* ("blind fish"), both dishes made from ingredients that have nothing to do with rabbits or fish. One wonders why Haldeman did not catch this. Furthermore, Haldeman knew nothing about the

Westphalian origins of the term *Panhas,* or that this was in fact a Celtic noun derived from a cooking vessel. But he did vindicate himself by observing that the terms *scrapple* and *Panhas* were interchangeable or, as he put it, "used cojointly." For all the subtle variations among recipes, and for all the perceived differences between Philadelphia versus country scrapple, Haldeman was basically right.

Haldeman's observation was echoed by many other contemporary writers interested in things Pennsylvania Dutch. In the dialect dictionary of Edward H. Rauch, otherwise known as *Rauch's Pennsylvania Dutch Hand-Book, Panhas* is translated as scrapple.[40] Rauch was not convinced, however, that Haldeman was correct in viewing *Pennsylfaanisch* as a transplanted dialect; rather, he considered it a product of New World evolution, a conclusion generally held by most linguists today. This same argument could be extended to scrapple, since it evolved along much different lines than its European counterpart once it was exposed to New World conditions. In short, it has undergone such thorough Americanization that cultural boundaries have become blurred; there are even Native American peoples who claim it as an aboriginal dish.

But there is an even more curious twist to this story, a twist that certainly would have confounded Haldeman and Rauch: Westphalian *Panhas* appeared in a well-known German cookbook reprinted in Milwaukee in 1879. The recipe was originally published by Henrietta Davidis, one of the most famous and prolific German cookbook writers of the nineteenth century.

The daughter of a village minister, Davidis was born in the Lower Rhineland in the heart of *Panhas* country. She died in 1876, but her most important cookbook continued in print under various editors until the 1940s. This was the bestselling classic called *Praktisches Kochbuch für die gewöhnliche und feinere Küche* (Practical Cookbook for Common and Refined Kitchens), which first appeared in 1845 under a different title. The book underwent a number of editorial mutations and grew in size over the years. It had a fundamental effect on the way *Panhas* recipes were presented in German cookbooks after that time. Davidis had been daring enough to publish a cookbook on the preparation of horse meat in 1848; she was hardly intimidated by old-time *Panhas,* which she tamed and reinvented as a middle-class dish made in part with beef. Her gentrified recipe appears in the accompanying sidebar with Americanized measurements.

Davidis's "Half-and-Half" Panhas

Panhas is best if you add half beef and half somewhat fatty pork, therefore you can prepare it according to taste for the former as well as the latter meats. Boil the meat until quite tender, carefully pick out all the little bones, then cut it into large cubes. Chop very fine and bring to a boil in the cooking broth which has been strained through a fine sieve. Season this with salt, pepper, cloves and allspice. While stirring continuously, sprinkle in as much good quality buckwheat flour (wheat flour cannot be used here) so that the mixture, after boiling up and cooking for $1/2$ to $3/4$ of an hour, becomes quite stiff and pulls from the pan. Then fill well scrubbed, oven-dried earthenware bowls and store in a cool, airy place.

The proportion of buckwheat flour to meat depends upon how vigorously the *Panhas* should be cooked. However, a good proportion for a flavorful *Panhas* is as follows: 2 pounds of fatty beef without bones, about $3^1/2$ quarts of the stock in which the meat was boiled, and 1 pound of buckwheat flour. It ought not be too lightly seasoned.

From Henriette Davidis, *Praktisches Kochbuch für die Deutschen in Amerika* (Milwaukee, 1879), 357–58. Translation by William Woys Weaver. A cross reference to frying *Panhas* has been omitted. *Note:* The meat is cubed in this recipe because Davidis presumed that a hand-turned meat chopper would be used to process the meat; diced meat is easier to feed into the blades.

As Davidis noted in the recipe, the addition of beef would make the dish more appealing to those who liked beef more than pork without putting off pork lovers. She also eliminated pork blood and in the end went so far as to suggest using beef altogether. This alteration was aimed at urban readers whose rising income at that time was allowing them to shift to a meat-centered diet rather than remain attached to the old gruel-and-vegetable diet of country living. Furthermore, northern Germany was undergoing an agricultural change during the mid-nineteenth century, with the introduction of large-scale dairy operations.[41] With the huge multiplication of dairy cattle came the availability of cheap beef as a salable by-product of the German cheese and butter industry. Davidis was well aware of this, and her long-lasting effect on such basic regional identity foods as *Panhas* is nowhere better demonstrated than in the professional butcher's recipe from Johann Jakob Weber's *Universal-Lexikon der Kochkunst*

(Universal Lexicon of Cookery) on page 18. A similar shift was taking place in the United States, with the appearance of beef scrapples in the Midwest. The keyword on both sides of the Atlantic was *industrialization*, and with it came a fundamental change in the way scrapple was viewed as food.

The Industrialization of Scrapple

The oldest scrapple maker still in business is Hemp's in Jefferson, Maryland. The business was founded in 1849 and represents the kind of small-scale family firms that characterized scrapple making for much of the nineteenth century—and even to this day. But market constraints are changing the profiles of many of these old firms. Hemp's no longer makes scrapple themselves; they purchase it by the pan from Shuff's of Thurmont, Maryland. However, in regions close to large cities like Philadelphia, Baltimore, and New York, there was an economic incentive to take scrapple making to a higher level. A key factor was the industrialization of the slaughtering and meat-packing business taking place in the Midwest, and true to a pattern repeated down through history, war was the strongest stimulus for change.

The Habbersett Brothers, of Middletown, Delaware County, Pennsylvania, are often credited with industrializing scrapple production. The firm was at one time the best known of all the scrapple makers in the Philadelphia region. It is still in business, although now owned as a subsidiary of a company in Wisconsin. The firm was established in 1863 by Joshua Habbersett, and at the height of its commercial activity, it employed some 130 people. While Habbersett is considered the first firm to produce scrapple on a large commercial scale, many other firms in various parts of the country, especially in the Midwest, quickly joined the market by the 1870s. In the Mid-Atlantic region, Joseph Obert (1865), of Lehighton, Pennsylvania; A. Darlington Strode (1883), at Strode's Mill, Chester County, Pennsylvania; Margerum's Scrapple Company in Trenton, New Jersey; Arbogast & Bastian of Allentown, Pennsylvania; and Allen's, of Media, Pennsylvania, were major players in the scrapple business. Aside from Habbersett's, Strode's is the only one of these companies to survive, although it is now a product line of Weaver's in Lebanon, Pennsylvania.

Strode's evolved over several generations, going back to Francis Strode (1805–90), a Quaker breeder of sheep and Chester White pigs.

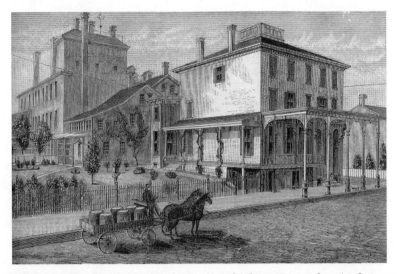

The Obert commercial slaughterhouse in Lehighton, Pennsylvania, from an 1884 wood engraving. The Obert family lived in the house in front of the business. ROUGHWOOD COLLECTION

He maintained a stand in Philadelphia's old Market Street Shambles, and later in the Reading Terminal Market. The Strode stall at the Reading Terminal Market was the firm's primary outlet, and it was well known for its fine fixtures, large mirrors, wooden display cases, and other attractive appointments. Like most early scrapple makers, Strode's also sold a general line of meats and sausages, and for many years in the 1890s, maintained a large orchard that was noted for its high-quality fruit. In 1900, the building at Strode's Mill was converted to steam manufacturing, and this greatly enlarged the output of scrapple so that by the 1920s, Strode's became one of the best-known brands on the market. On the other hand,

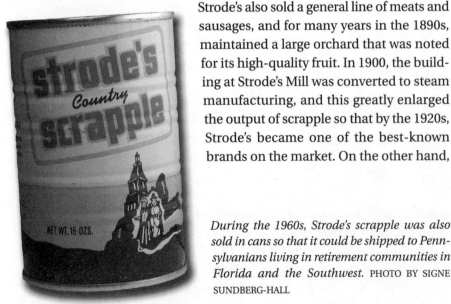

During the 1960s, Strode's scrapple was also sold in cans so that it could be shipped to Pennsylvanians living in retirement communities in Florida and the Southwest. PHOTO BY SIGNE SUNDBERG-HALL

William Ellesworth Hickman (1863–1940) in a photo by W. F. Grubb, West Chester, Pennsylvania, 1889. Hickman used an inheritance from Coatesville, Pennsylvania, ironworks owner Rebecca Lukens to expand his business in Pocopson, Chester County, Pennsylvania. ROUGHWOOD COLLECTION

most of the Strode pork was locally raised, and Strode's never made the quantum leap to large-scale slaughtering like Habbersett's.

Joshua Habbersett launched his business during the darkest years of the Civil War, when there was a definite shortage of farm labor and an overabundance of surplus pork products from an industry then devoted to mess pork and military rations. The U.S. economy was under enormous stress, so his mass production of an inexpensive meat substitute may be viewed along similar lines to the popularity of Spam during World War II. A critical element in this development was the ability of the railroads to ship western-raised pigs to eastern markets. Habbersett's pigs were not locally raised. Most of the large-scale commercial scrapple makers were located along railroads, and this applied as well to many of the middling-size businesses like my great-grandfather's in Chester County, Pennsylvania.

That firm was called Joseph P. Hickman and Sons, and it belonged to a group of small-scale Chester County scrapple makers that included J. L. Entrinken, Edward Gibson, Percy Hoopes (whose scrapple sauce recipe is provided on page 91), Jackson & Hines, and others. Joseph Pennock Hickman (1836–1921), of Thornbury, Delaware County, Pennsylvania, began the firm, although in many respects, his pork-butchering business traced back to Thomas Cheney Hickman (1809–41), who according to family tradition sent scrapple to the Philadelphia market. Joseph Hickman's son, William Ellesworth (1863–1940), relocated the business along Pocopson Creek in the 1890s and used a spur of the Wilmington-Reading railroad line to service his slaughterhouse. None of the buildings, not even his old

stone farmhouse, remain standing today. But in 1983, my grandmother offered these valuable insights into the business and its
method of operation:

> My father [William Ellesworth Hickman] was a pork butcher, specializ-
> ing in salted pork, stuffed hams, scrapple, and various cuts of meat. His
> employees were black and lived in stone cottages near our house in
> Pocopson; all that is gone now, even the railroad spur which brought
> the pigs in from the West. Papa gave his employees the snouts, ears,
> tails, and lights because he did not put them in his scrapple. His men
> made scrapple in two hundred-gallon kettles which Papa called scrap-
> ple pots. They were so big that the wood-burning stoves had to be built
> up around them. The stoves were made of brick. He had enough of
> these kettles to cook five or six pigs at a time, and the skins went in. The
> men used a long paddle to stir the scrapple; it looked like a laundry pad-
> dle, only bigger and slightly tongued. Old people in the area called those
> paddles mundles, but I do not know what that word means. Papa sea-
> soned his scrapple with sage.[42]

William Hickman's scrapple was sold primarily in the
Wilmington, Delaware, and Reading, Pennsylvania, markets because he was linked to the railroad connecting
those two cities. He also shipped scrapple by trolley from
Lenape, Pennsylvania, to West Chester, where he maintained a stand at the farmers' market, an elaborate brick
building demolished some years ago. Without those rail
connections, his business could not have survived
because he could not compete with scrapple makers
closer to Philadelphia. In flavor and texture, his scrapple was similar to a distinctive old-style scrapple still
made by Leidy's, a firm established in 1893 at Souderton, Pennsylvania.

The popularity of commercial scrapple increased
considerably after the Civil War because it filled an
important dietary niche for urban workers: a food
that reminded them of their country roots, but
that they could no longer make themselves. This

*Tiger maple mundle from Nuremberg, Schuylkill County,
Pennsylvania, c. 1840–60. This heavy-duty pot stick
measures 18½ inches long.* EX. ROBACKER COLLECTION,
ROUGHWOOD COLLECTION

Habbersett's scrapple is sold in a distinctive wrapping so that it can be easily spotted at meat counters. PHOTO BY DON YODER

connectedness was further reinforced by the sale of commercially made scrapple by restaurants specializing in breakfast menus, by Horn & Hardart cafeterias during the early 1900s, and by the growth of diners during the interwar period.

Nostalgia has always played a role in scrapple served in urban settings, and the nostalgic lament raised by the food media was great when the Habbersett dynasty came to an end only a few years after the demise of Strode's. In 1985, after years of feuding among the Habbersetts over the management of their business, the firm was sold to Johnsonville Foods of Sheboygan, Wisconsin, and then resold in 1988 to Jones Dairy Farm of Fort Atkinson, Wisconsin. The company continues to operate as a division of Jones Dairy Farm at Folcroft, Pennsylvania, but it no longer commands the local market presence it once enjoyed. This may be due to the perception that the recipe has been changed, though Habbersett's says otherwise; the most common grumbling in the Philadelphia area is that Habbersett's does not taste the way it used to—but it still gets high marks for texture. However, Jones Dairy Farm is itself an old firm (established in 1889), and with its national marketing networks, the company has managed to place the Habbersett's name in many stores across the country.

Jones Dairy Farm also purchased the Rapa Scrapple Company in Bridgeville, Delaware, in 1981 and has marketed those products in tandem with the Habbersett's label. More recently, the Rapa Scrapple Company has received a large amount of publicity, since its product is one of the featured elements in the annual Apple-Scrapple Festival begun in 1992 at Bridgeville. Usually held the second weekend in October, the first festival attracted about twenty-five hundred people; attendance has now ballooned to about forty thousand. Elsewhere in the country, similar scrapple-oriented promotional events have sprouted up, such as scrapple carving, scrapple throwing, and scrapple recipe competitions.

Detailed profiles of America's leading scrapple makers would fill a very large book, and the recipes they use are as varied and individualistic as the butchers themselves. One other company does merit mention, as it is a reminder that Baltimore is as much a scrapple town as Philadelphia. Henry Green Parks Jr. (1917–89), an African-American, began Parks Sausage Company in Baltimore in 1951. He converted an old dairy plant and soon put himself in open competition with firms like Rapa, which was essentially a Baltimore label. "More Parks sausages, Mom," on radio advertisements is still remembered by many people today. The well-known Parks scrapple was the only African-American brand to become a household word on a regional level.

The Great Scrapple Diaspora

While passing from Harrisburg, Pennsylvania, to Pittsburgh by canal boat in 1842, Charles Dickens remarked on the meal that was served both for supper and breakfast: "At about six o'clock all the small tables were put together to form one long table, and everybody sat down to tea, coffee, bread, butter, salmon, shad, liver, steak, potatoes, pickles, ham, chops, black puddings, and sausages."[43] The "black pudding" he

referred to was undoubtedly scrapple, although he did not know it by that name (nor did he bother to ask). Scrapple, not blood pudding, was a common item on canal boat and steamboat menus throughout the 1800s, because it was cheap and could be prepared quickly in the cramped quarters of a floating kitchen. In the heyday of the Pennsylvania Railroad, scrapple was also served in the dining cars as well as in the train station cafés. But the greatest mover of scrapple into the hinterlands of America was migration, because wherever Pennsylvanians settled, they took traditional scrapple making with them.

Wrought iron scrapple turner made in Carlisle, Pennsylvania, about 1800. These short-handled spatulas were used for frying mush and scrapple on the hot surface of a ten-plate stove. ROUGHWOOD COLLECTION

Pawnhas

Purchase the "jowls" of a hog from your butcher together with a liver and heart. Boil all until very tender. Take out all bones, chop the heart and meat from the jowls until very fine. Crumble the liver as finely as possible and put all back into the kettle. Now season with pepper and salt, and be sure to add enough water to keep it from being too rich or greasy. Stir in white corn meal until you have a thin mush, let cook slowly half an hour, pour into a large crock or jar. Set away to cool. When cold, slice like mush and put into a skillet to fry. Add no grease. This is delicious and will keep indefinitely in a cool place.

From *Cooking Club Magazine*, February 1906.

During the early 1800s, the Pennsylvania Dutch introduced scrapple into Ontario, Canada, and many regions of the Midwest. It can still be found in any of the numerous Amish and Mennonite neighborhoods of Ohio, Indiana, Illinois, Wisconsin, Kansas, and Iowa. Scrapple also appeared in regional cookbooks, such as *Practical Housekeeping*, which by 1884 sold over two hundred thousand copies and included three very different scrapple recipes.[44] Likewise, mass-market journals began publishing regional recipes in an effort to promote American dishes.

The *Cooking Club Magazine* for February 1906 featured Pennsylvania Dutch *Panhas*, but under the presumption that all the meat ingredients would be bought from a butcher.[45] The recipe is given above because it is one of the oldest printed recipes to come from the Pennsylvania Dutch community. Its western Maryland or Valley of Virginia origin is evident in the use of white cornmeal, the term *hog jowls*, and especially the colloquial spelling of *Pawnhas*.

Butchers still sell scrapple in midwestern farm markets (some are listed at the back of this book), and large numbers of people still make it at home. But scrapple is also found in areas settled later by immigrants who came directly from Germany, especially in Chicago, parts of Wisconsin, and Missouri. Some groups brought with them a type of oatmeal scrapple called *götta* or goetta, which is popular in the Ohio counties south of Toledo and north of Cincinnati, as well as in parts of northern Kentucky. If a general statement can be made about the westward spread of scrapple, it hopped, skipped, and jumped across the heartland until it reached the Rocky Mountains. That is where the scrapple "diaspora" officially stops. The recipe for Venison Scrapple on page 105, traveled from Pennsylvania to Colorado in the early 1900s and represents this later phase in the further Americanization of the dish. In fact, in Colorado, it was often made with antelope.

Some of the dispersion of scrapple across America also must be credited to Sarah Tyson Rorer (1849–1937), who was asked to promote corn-based recipes at the Columbian Exposition in Chicago during 1893. Although she was of Pennsylvania Dutch background—the Tysons were among those first thirteen families from Crefeld to settle Germantown in the 1680s—Rorer did not like scrapple or any kind of countrified dish that smacked of backwardness and rustic sensibilities. As the head of the Philadelphia Cooking School and author of numerous books, Rorer considered herself a progressive cook, performing her culinary arts on a stage in elaborate lace dresses just to demonstrate that scientific cookery was also impeccably neat. But scrapple did prove useful when it came to turning her science into dollars, and she was above all else a pragmatic and practical woman.

She took charge of the Illinois Corn Exhibit at the exposition, and in the model kitchen set up on a stage, she demonstrated recipes each day of the week. In connection with the corn dishes, a small fifteen-page pamphlet cookbook was distributed to those who attended the presentations. Recipes included Zuni Indian breads, a number of southern cornbreads, various hominy dishes, cornmeal mush, and scrapple.[46] According to Emma Weigley, Rorer's biographer, more than 250,000 copies of the corn booklet were given away, and some were even sent to Japan and Europe.[47] If this huge number of scrapple recipes put into general circulation were not enough, Helen Louise Johnson, editor of *Table Talk* magazine in Philadelphia, published her own version of scrapple in the June 1894 issue, in response to a request from a reader in St. Paul, Minnesota.[48] The timing of this request would suggest that Rorer had left a definite impression on the Midwest. Rorer never published her recipe anywhere else, although it was often copied without attribution, but Johnson's recipe was included in *Table Talk's Cook Book* in 1897, and then assumed a life of its own in a little booklet she wrote for a local manufacturing company.[49] These two scrapple recipes appeared over and over in the cooking literature of the early 1900s, and many manuscript recipes for scrapple can be traced to these two sources.

Cover of the fifth edition of The Enterprising Housekeeper *(1906)*. ROUGHWOOD
COLLECTION

If history is capable of subjecting
little ironies on posterity, then it
did so in the Illinois Corn Exhibit,
because the cornmeal Rorer used in
all her recipes, including scrapple,
came from the firm of William Lea
& Sons of Wilmington, Delaware,
owned by a nephew of Elizabeth
Ellicott Lea. But the story becomes
much more convoluted than that.
Helen Louise Johnson's scrapple
recipe was actually "invented" for
a newfangled kitchen device that
changed the way people prepared
homemade scrapple ever since.
This was the crank-turned meat chopper, patented by the Enterprise
Manufacturing Company of Philadelphia in the 1880s. Helen Louise
Johnson developed her scrapple recipe for the instruction booklet that
was included with every Enterprise meat chopper sold in the country.

Johnson's recipes were eventually gathered and published in an
Enterprise promotional cookbook called *The Enterprising Housekeeper,* which first appeared in 1896. This cookbook was available for
sale in every store that offered Enterprise products, and it proved to
be extremely popular at the bargain price of 25 cents. It went through
numerous editions, each one with Johnson's scrapple recipe promi-
nently positioned in the section on meats. In between the recipes
were advertisements devoted to various Enterprise "money-saving"
products, from sadirons to ice shredders, meat juicers, and coffee
mills. Not only was Enterprise one of the first firms to introduce the
idea of a kitchen gadget for every task, but Johnson's little cookbook
also accomplished two very important things: It brought the industrialization of meat processing into the average American kitchen,
and it changed the way scrapple was made. With a meat chopper, the
housewife did not need to start with an animal carcass. She did not
need to live on a farm. She could shop at a market to find what she

The Enterprise meat chopper was designed for mounting to the top of a kitchen table. ROUGHWOOD COLLECTION

wanted. She could grind up whatever bits and pieces of meat suited her fancy. In fact, she could make scrapple from the leftovers of yesterday's dinner. With that, scrapple graduated to home economy.

Scrapple as the Frugal Food Alternative

Laura Shapiro has exposed some of the humorous and bizarre sidelights of this supposedly scientific cookery in *Perfection Salad,* her classic study of turn-of-the-century American culinary reformers. For many of these women, meat loaf was the Utopian answer to scrapple. Others simply tamed scrapple with new culinary weapons like the hand-cranked meat chopper, creating such oddities as scrapple croquets, scrapple timbales, scrapple puffs, and scrapple stuffed and baked in peppers. In its attempt to force scrapple into the mold of high-class cookery, not only did the reform movement introduce new and strange ingredients, but its advocates also standardized the dish so that all scrapples made with the choppers resembled one another in texture. The net effect was a lot like the introduction of Cuisinart in the 1970s: Food was subjected to yet another form of homogenization. At the time, the emphasis was not on the effects of processing, but on the convenience of making small-batch recipes quickly, and on saving money by finding new ways to cook leftovers.

A case in point would be Frances Owens's 1903 *Mrs. Owens' Cook Book,* which contains a recipe for Philadelphia scrapple in a section devoted to dishes like minced mutton, Union hash, and fish cakes— all of them based on grinding up leftovers. The recipe came from Harford, Susquehanna County, Pennsylvania, and called for "bits of cold fowl or any kind of cold meat, or 2 or 3 kinds together." This mixed meat hash was boiled, then thickened with cornmeal and molded like any other scrapple recipe. It lacked herbs and spices, and made no mention of buckwheat, which is (or should be) one of the defining ingredients in any Philadelphia-style scrapple. Yet from a historical standpoint, the recipe does provide a literary model for the Clam Scrapple on page 86 and Ham Scrapple on page 89.

The popularity of these small-batch scrapples made with nontraditional ingredients was especially strong in turn-of-the-century charitable cookbooks throughout the industrialized parts of the country. The 1911 *Catskill Cook Book,* an upstate New York cookbook issued by a local church, featured a recipe for beef scrapple that also appeared in several other cookbooks of this type prior to World War I. In the class-conscious eyes of reformist cooks, beef was a far more progressive and much less uncouth alternative to the poverty associations of old-fashioned country pork. This preference for beef has stayed with homemade scrapples ever since, but it also changed the character and purpose of the dish, just as it did in industrialized Germany.

Food shortages during World War I encouraged further experimentation with scrapple, especially dishes that did not use meat. Period magazines are full of these scrapple adaptations, perhaps the most avant garde being the nut scrapples promoted by Marion Harris Neil, who was for several years the cooking editor of the *Ladies' Home Journal.* Her *Thrift Cook Book* was designed to deal with wartime shortages, although it finally

One of a series of recipe pamphlets utilizing meat leftovers. Chicago, c. 1948.

Nut Scrapple

Stir two cups corn meal, one cup of hominy, and two table-spoons of salt into twelve cups boiling water and cook thoroughly until soft. Remove from the fire, add three cups chopped nut meats, one-fourth teaspoon pepper and one-eighth teaspoon powdered cloves, and pour while hot into a greased pan. Sliced and fried or broiled, this takes the place of meat and furnishes an appetizing dish.

From Marion Harris Neil, *The Thrift Cook Book* (1919), 339.

---

came out after the war was over. The Nut Scrapple recipe from this book, given above, is probably most flavorful when made with hickory nuts or hazelnuts. Pecans would make a good substitute. The recipe is also conveniently vegan, so it would be acceptable to vegetarians as well as Jews. In fact, nut and bean scrapples were served in several Kosher vegetarian restaurants in New York and Philadelphia during this same period, as surviving menus attest.

The Jewish community in Philadelphia, one of the oldest in the country, has always coexisted with scrapple. As a result, there were innumerable roundabout recipes that skirted the issue of pork. In this category falls chicken scrapple. One of the more recent recipes was widely circulated during the 1970s by the Pen Argyl Milling Company in the Pocono Mountains, using the firm's buckwheat groats (kasha). Their kasha-chicken scrapple was served at several Jewish resorts in the Catskills as well as Atlantic City.

The problem of leftovers was not only a concern for housekeepers. Resorts and restaurants continually faced the need to recycle unused or unserved meat. That issue was addressed in Alice Easton's 1940 *Recipes and Menus for Restaurant Profit,* whereby leftover Thanksgiving and Christmas turkeys were converted into turkey scrapple and thus an added source of income. This simple solution to the annual question of what do with that old turkey carcass seemed so appealing to the editors of *American Cooking* that they published Easton's recipe in the February 1941 issue.[50] The timing was perfect, because as soon as World War II broke out, scrapple again came to the fore as an alternative food to get through times of shortage. Turkey scrapple still has its merits, and it is being sold commercially not just as an alternative to pork, but also as a health food. Turkey scrapple is no different from any other, however: It is only as healthful as the ingredients put into it. But if health is to be the focus, then scrapples made with oats, which help block the uptake of cholesterol, could benefit greatly from this marketing angle.

A Homey Dish Called Goetta

Scrapple and *Panhas* were not the only pork-and-meal preparations to spread into the Midwest. During the nineteenth century, especially after the German immigrations of 1848, a north German relative of *Panhas* was brought to Ohio by farmers from the general area of Osnabrück and Oldenburg, which lie to the east of Westphalia. In the cold, swampy marshlands of that part of Germany, oats were the grain of choice, and they figured in a wide range of dishes, including a type of loose scrapple called *götta,* meaning groats—hulled, cracked grain. The standard High German term is *Grütze* (plural), a cognate with English grits. As with Westphalian *Panhas,* ingredients varied from one region to the next, and a large amount of ethnographic research has been collected on the subject—enough for a book. The general pattern was simple: Pork scrapple was made with coarse oatmeal rather than with buckwheat or other flours. Otherwise, *götta* and *Panhas* were essentially the same in concept. The one main difference, however, is that true farmhouse *götta* was generally eaten as a loose porridge, scooped up with a piece of bread. In this respect, it retains a more medieval character, although when cold, it stiffens up like scrapple.

The Ohio settlers who made *götta* spoke a distinct dialect of *Plattdeutsch* (Low German) and settled primarily in areas around Cincinnati and Toledo. Many people in rural Ohio still make the dish under the name "German scrapple" but often use ground beef instead of pork products, since beef is cheap and readily available in supermarkets. The center of local identity is unquestionably Cincinnati, where German slaughterhouses in the nineteenth century provided ready ingredients for making the dish on a relatively large scale. The word *götta* has been transliterated into English as *goetta,* and a search on the Internet for recipes under this name will yield quite a large number of websites, most of them in southern Ohio or northern Kentucky. Several writers interested in local foods have taken up the cause for goetta, among

Glier's goetta labeling and packaging also include the family coat-of-arms.

them Linda Stradley, whose *I'll Have What They're Having* (2002) provides both descriptive comments and methods of preparation.

Although it is not well known outside Ohio, goetta is not in danger of disappearing. Glier's Meats in Covington, Kentucky, has been promoting the dish for many years and even helped establish the USDA standard for identifying commercially made goetta. Glier's also changed the texture of goetta so that the commercial product is stiff and easily sliced like commercial scrapple. It is sold in a package resembling a large sausage. Glier family enthusiasm for the dish has led them to sponsor an annual goetta festival in Covington, which, like the Apple-Scrapple Festival in Delaware, is now well known throughout the region. The only trick to making goetta is using the right kind of oatmeal: It must be pinhead or steal-cut. This is the secret to goetta's unique texture. Since so many goetta recipes are available from the Cincinnati area, on page 88 I have included a recipe from the Scheffer family of Woodville, Ohio, which is southeast of Toledo. Much of that neighborhood was German-speaking until World War I.

Scrapple in the South

Many Americans do not associate scrapple with the South, but in fact, it is—or was—as common there as anywhere else. In fact, aside from the ubiquitous liver pudding and liver mush, there seem to be a great many more regional variations and highly localized names than in the

North. In 1949, the American linguist Raven McDavid compiled a list of southern words applied to scrapple and scrapplelike dishes, all of them garnered from interviews with impoverished families, for scrapple in the South is most definitely a poverty food—one reason it is rarely mentioned in so-called plantation cookbooks. The list includes *ponhoss* (Newberry County, South Carolina, and Dekalb County, Georgia); *purkle* (DeKalb County, Georgia); rice pudding or liver mush with rice (Williamsburg and Georgetown Counties, South Carolina); scrabblin' mush (Richland County, South Carolina); and white pudding, for liver pudding (St. Johns County, Florida).[51]

McDavid only scratched the surface of his material, because many more terms have come to light since then. Yet certain patterns do emerge: *Ponhoss* is most certainly associated with early frontier migrations, when Germans from Pennsylvania and Maryland moved south down the Piedmont. *Purkle (Pörkel)* is also a German word, but it was generally applied to something brined; it evidently has become detached from the original food and applied to a highly localized preparation. Liver mush with rice is a common Coastal Carolina dish, and scrabblin' mush connects us with a Low Country version of Appalachian poor-do. The Florida reference to liver pudding as "white" echoes vocabularies also common in Europe, as in the case of *witte balkenbrij* (white scrapple) in Holland, a scrapple that is "white" because it does not contain pork blood. McDavid did not ask his informants for working recipes, so we can only speculate about the scrapples to which these terms applied. But one thing is certain: Southerners did not use buckwheat; they used white cornmeal, hominy, or leftover rice—or all three.

Since I have provided a recipe for Scrabblin' Mush on page 99, I will not say much more about it than this: As a poverty food, it had no fixed recipe. It was created with any leftovers on hand in the kitchen, but when made with day-old rice, it was particularly popular among African-Americans. The word itself traces to Ulster Irish *scrippin* or *scrippins*, meaning leftovers.[52] The expression was probably a lot more widespread in popular speech than McDavid realized, shared as it was by both poor whites and blacks. Northern blacks made something similar called gypsy pie. It was called pie mainly because it was baked rather than boiled in a kettle. It consisted of cold rice or hominy grits mixed with beaten eggs, milk, finely chopped meat, pepper, salt, and butter, which was then baked in any sort of pan or pot available.[53] This

was a scrapplelike pudding from the 1920s reflecting the better economic condition of blacks who migrated North for work.

The South also produced a variety of dishes associated with pork
butchering and scrapple making that do not appear in the North. One
of the most distinctive was backbone pie, which employed the chine,
normally boiled in the North for its scrapple meat. A recipe for this pie
is given in the accompanying sidebar because of its rarity in printed
form. Part of the pork chine is boiled, then baked in a deep-dish pie
similar to pot pie. It was served as a main dish during hog butchering.

Published scrapple recipes do appear in southern cookbooks much
more frequently than most people realize. Scrapple was and still is made
in pockets all over the South, but the most fascinating recipe is probably that of Annabella P. Hill, who lived most of her life in western Georgia. She wrote a cookbook in 1867, which ran through several editions
and is now considered the culinary Bible of the Reconstruction South.
Her recipe for "scraffle" in the accompanying sidebar was missed by H.
L. Mencken and others fascinated with the linguistic permutations of
American speech. *Scraffle* is not a misspelling; Annabella had ample
opportunity to correct it if it had been. The word is perfectly acceptable
Georgia dialect, and doubtless it finds a close kinship to other scrapple
terms like scrabblin' mush. The best part of Hill's recipe is that she wrote
it from firsthand experience; it was not a recipe she copied from a
source far removed from LaGrange, Georgia, where she lived.

Later on in the century, scrapple recipes appeared with regularity
in fund-raising or charitable cookbooks. The recipes reflect an interest in either home economics or the larger world of women's maga-

---

Backbone Pie

Take the small end of the backbone, cut in pieces two or three
inches long, wash well and boil in water until done. Have ready a
nice pastry; line a baking dish with some of the pastry, lay the
bones into this dish with some of the water in which they were
boiled. Season to taste with salt and pepper, adding butter and a
few pieces of pastry dropped here and there in the pie. Cover the
top of the dish with pastry; place in a stove; bake nice and brown.

This is a great Southern dish, and delicious when nicely prepared.

From Virginia E. James, *Mother James' Key to Good Cooking* (New York, 1892), 80.

Mrs. Hill's Georgia Scraffle

Boil a fresh-killed hog's head tender. This is made in the winter during what we at the South call "hog-killing." Take it up and remove all the bones; chop the meat very fine and season it with salt, pepper, and sage, as sausage meat; strain the liquor; wipe out the pot nicely; return the broth to the pot; there should be about a quart of this. Put the meat back and stir into the broth fine corn meal until the mass is the consistence of soft mush; let this simmer half an hour, stirring frequently; pour the mixture into pans three or four inches deep. When cold, slice in thin slices, roll in corn meal or flour, and fry in boiling lard, a light brown.

From Annabella P. Hill, *Mrs. Hill's New Cook Book* (New York, 1872), 63.

zines. For example, a Philadelphia scrapple recipe was included in a small cookbook issued in 1910 by the Stephenson Mission Band, associated with the Presbyterian church in Abingdon, Virginia, on the Tennessee border, a region where poor-do and liver pudding were made by folks up in the hills.[54] Many of the other recipes in this cookbook trace to popular mass-market journals of the period, so bona fide Philadelphia-style scrapple was probably viewed as something exotic and up-to-date—it was already a standard item on the cafeteria menu of the fabled Horn & Hardart's up North.

What is interesting about southern cookbooks from the early 1900s is the total lack of traditional poverty recipes. They were swept under the rug of progressive cookery, only to surface anecdotally in reminiscences and ethnographic studies. The cultural divide between northern and southern ideas about scrapple cookery is probably best illustrated by an often-repeated tale about feeding the poor in a down-and-out Appalachian community during the Depression. The story, told by G. W. Stauffer of Charlottesville, Virginia, bears repeating. It appeared in the *Pennsylvania Dutchman* of March 1, 1953, and described an event that occurred at Rockwood, Roane County, Tennessee.

During the winter of 1932 I was living in Rockwood, a small town in Tennessee. A feed warehouse and farm owner decided that the quickest way to dispose of an oversupply of hogs was to slaughter them and retail the parts for what he could get for them. He spread the parts on tables in his feed warehouse. The call went out, "Pick out what you like and give me what is right."

I quickly bargained for several heads, livers, etc. A friend met me as I was on my way home. Said he: "Yankee, where you all going with them pig jowls? I thought that was a Southern dish." I agreed that he was right, but I told him these heads were to be cooked into a dish for a man who wanted to eat long and fast; they would be served on the table as Ponhaws or Scrapple.

"Come over to the house tomorrow evening," I said to my friend, "maybe it gives a metzelsoup."

He came and we gave him a liberal portion. The next evening he returned with several friends. Their proposition was this: There were several hundred families in that town in which the head of the family had been out of work for some time. So many were short of food. The warehouse man would contribute those heads, livers, feet, etc. The business men of the town would supply the balance of the supplies. Would I supervise the preparing and cooking of Ponhaws?

Some delivered a load of wood, others contributed cornmeal, flour, salt, pepper, three cast iron kettles. The blacksmith made stirring irons. We put five to work with knifes, cutting up the heads. I started the pots boiling.

Then we sent word around to the town, "Come and get it!" They came, with dishpans, cook pots, and pans, or what they had. Each was told to let it cool overnight, then slice it and fry it on a griddle.

Some came back within an hour. "It war no use to let it cool and then make hit hot again, it's good to eat now," they said.

That was Ponhaws cooking as you never saw before. Five days. The heads, livers, hearts, and feet from eighty hogs! And we scraped the last kettle to the bottom.

The narrator was originally from York County, Pennsylvania, so that is why he knew all about scrapple making and the *Metzelsupp* food gift. Most interesting was the reaction of the Tennessee locals, who had never seen the dish before. They ate it fresh, as a hot porridge, just as peasants had done in the Middle Ages. They had none of the modern feigned squeamishness about scrapple, because they had no cultural prejudices against pork, the mainstay of the southern diet. Not the least, it resembled something they already knew: poor-do and liver mush.

Liver Mush and Liver Pudding:
An Icon Food of the Carolinas

If you happen to get arrested in North Carolina, you are most likely to be served liver mush and grits as jailhouse rations. Liver mush three times a day is the Tarheel idea of culinary paradise. And local cookbooks, like *Jim Graham's Farm Family Cookbook for City Folks* (2002), will gladly tell you how to make it. "Liver mush fills the need," to quote one North Carolinian I recently interviewed as he helped himself to his third LLT (liver mush, lettuce, and tomato sandwich). "A right large need." This is indeed a food that comforts.

Cleveland County, North Carolina, claims to be the heartland of Carolina liver mush country. This may change because, due to its nutritional benefits, liver mush is undergoing something of a revival, and younger producers are popping up in many other parts of the state. It is also appearing on local menus with such novel combinations as liver mush and feta cheese omelet. Indeed, the list of creations is growing daily, spurred on no doubt by the annual Liver Mush Expo, begun in 1987 by Mack's of Shelby, North Carolina. Let us simply say that there is liver mush and there is liver mush—the variations are many. A discerning Tarheel can tell the difference between the homemade and the commercial product, as well as the highly sought-after "dishpan liver mush," which has chunkier meat. According to USDA regulations, commercially produced liver mush must contain at least 30 percent pork liver in addition to other pork products. Like scrapple, it is commonly thickened with cornmeal. All else is variable, such as the addition of onions, ample doses of black pepper, sage, or some other herb flavoring. Corriher's hot liver mush, made in Landis, North Carolina, contains spicy red pepper, and this new twist is proving to be quite popular.

The accepted history of North Carolina liver mush is that it is a food dispersed southward by migrations from Pennsylvania. The fact that it is a scrapple thickened with cereal (normally cornmeal) further strengthens the idea of this link, especially since the North Carolina Piedmont was settled by Pennsylvania Quakers and a large number of Germans. But all across the South, there is a "hog pudding" tradition that may ultimately derive from the English rather than the Pennsylvania Germans. Wright's *English Dialect Dictionary* is fairly clear in assigning a narrow range of meanings to the term *hog pudding*: pork sausage, a black pudding, or a sausage made with blood and meat. This is also confirmed by English cookbook literature.

John Nott's 1726 *Cooks and Confectioners Dictionary* provided a recipe for a hog's pudding using umbles, lights, heart, and "all the flesh about them," boiled tender and minced together with the liver. This hash was thickened with egg yolks, cream, wine, spices, and hog's fat, then put up in a gut like a sausage.[55] The end product was a rich preparation intended for the tables of the gentry and high nobility, yet the first part of the recipe reads like the beginning step for liver mush. In short, folk cookery simplified elaborate models and changed them into new dishes out of economic expedience. This was typical of the process of Americanization and the utter simplicity of approach that characterizes so many liver mush recipes. The real problem lies in the confusing mix of terms applied to the dish, because while some people call it liver mush, others call it liver pudding, as in the case of the recipe from Virginia given below.

Technically speaking, the dish is liver pudding when it contains no cornmeal (like Pennsylvania Dutch *Lewwerwarscht*), but since both homemade liver pudding and liver mush were stored in crocks, they had a similar appearance. The mush can be sliced and fried like scrapple; the pudding falls apart when heated and is thus eaten like gravy. In the South, both are also eaten cold, usually sliced and served in a sandwich. The classic Tarheel accompaniment for fried liver mush is creamed corn, although there is also a school that prefers sorghum syrup.

From a historical standpoint, it is probably the liver pudding that served as the original food model for liver mush. The dish could be

Liver Pudding (Southwest Virginia)

This recipe comes from a seventy-four-year old resident of Rural Retreat, Virginia, who said she has been making it since she was twelve years old (1940). She never heard of it being called liver mush, but since she uses cornmeal to thicken the mixture, that is indeed what she makes. I reproduce her recipe verbatim as written:

Cook hog head with heart and "melts." When tender, pick meat off of the hogs head, grind that along with other meats. Let the broth cool, then take the fat off and pour enough of the broth over the meat to cover it.

Cook the mixture with cornmeal just long enough to get the cornmeal done. Chopped onion can be added here if you prefer. Salt to taste. Use just enough cornmeal so that when the mixture cools, it can be sliced. Pour the mixture into pans to cool (loaf pans work best). Slice.

found in Elizabethan England, it was known in colonial Virginia and Maryland, and it appears under many guises in several parts of the South. This diversity of recipes, like biodiversity in plants, is one indication that the dish did not come from some other part of the country, but rather evolved locally, adapting to whatever ingredients were available. A case in point would be the liver mush of South Carolina, which is commonly made with rice and has developed a number of distinctive forms.

One of these has recently come to light in Levy County, Florida, in an old recipe preserved by Onnie Lee Smoak (1883–1965), whose family originally came from the area of Orangeburg, South Carolina. She called the dish hog liver pudding, and it contained a head, two livers with lights, two hearts, two sweetbreads, and four kidneys, plus other meat, salt, pepper, and sage. If served hot like a porridge, it was mixed with cooked rice—a meal for those who helped with the hog butchering. If put up for later use, the pudding was stuffed in casings, boiled, and then smoked. The smoked liver pudding was baked in an oven until brown, and served with hot biscuits and syrup as the centerpiece of a special butchering day meal.[56] The Smoak recipe straddles several distinct hog liver traditions: a *Metzelsupp* for the guests after the manner of South Carolina scrabblin' mush, a large liver sausage of the sort once made by the Pennsylvania Dutch, and the unusual tradition of smoking it so that it could be baked and served like Pennsylvania Dutch *Seimawwe* (stuffed pig's stomach). Like many families in Orangeburg County, South Carolina, the Smoaks were of German background, and while the format of their butchering practices retained an echo of that past, the actual recipe was worked out in thoroughly southern terms.

Poor-Do and Burgoo: The Appalachian Scrapples

In *Smoky Mountain Voices* (1993), Harold Farwell listed the various places where the term *poor-do* is known, and most of those localities are in the general vicinity of eastern Kentucky, eastern Tennessee, and the western tips of North Carolina and Virginia. This is the same part of the country that has given us wild goose plums, "greasy beans," and cowpeas, called *crowders,* the last two of which can find their way into poor-do. The general character of poor-do is eclectic, but the word has a clear subsidiary meaning: meat, a one-pot meal, something more substantial than plain vegetables or mush, an expression that would certainly fit any sort of pudding meat.

The connection of the word with scrapple or liver pudding was made by Horace Kephart in his 1913 classic *Our Southern Highlanders,* a first-person account of his travels in southern Appalachia. It entered into his account in a chapter on mountain dialect, specifically a dish that was served to him with lath-open bread, a type of flaky, flat biscuit-bread made with buttermilk and soda.[57] It was Kephart who said that poor-do came from the Pennsylvania Germans who settled in the South, but since the structural makeup of the dish has been described so infrequently, this can be accepted only as conjecture. Kephart may or may not have been aware that the word appeared elsewhere a few years before he heard it. Poor-do figured in one of the reminiscences related by Tilatha Wilson English in the 1909 *Pioneer Days in the Southwest from 1850 to 1879.*

The preparation was mentioned in passing by Tilatha, who left Kentucky at the age of two, eventually settling with her parents in Texas in 1845. The reminiscences she wrote in 1909 dealt with her early life on the Texas frontier. H. L. Mencken and all the other American linguists who have recorded the term *poor-do* missed the critical point that Tilatha's family came from Kentucky, which underscores the fact that while it may have cropped up in other places, the term is essentially Appalachian in origin. Tilatha probably learned the word from her mother.

> We had no flour for several years, so we would stew our pumpkins till done and put it in meal and salt it, if we chanced to have salt, and work it up into a dough, making it into small thin cakes called pumpkin bread. When we had hog meat we would fry a few pieces, take the grease and crumble corn bread in it, putting in water and salt, and we had a pot of soup called "poor do." We thought it very good those days.[58]

It is clear from Tilatha's narrative that poor-do had four important features: meat or meat drippings, a cereal thickener (usually cornbread or cornmeal), and a thick, semiliquid consistency. The other critical feature was that the cold leftovers stiffened up like pudding and could be sliced and fried the next day for breakfast. In structure, it was a mixture made on the spot, and this is why the term probably derives from the Middle English verb *poure-to,* meaning to mix together.[59] Poor-do is also the immediate progenitor of the black dialect term *burgoo,* a word now associated almost exclusively with

Kentucky stews of complex mixture. Burgoo has undergone consid-erable reinvention at the hands of professional chefs and cookbook writers.[60] Part of its fame, at least in the United States, rests on its fes-tive associations with the Kentucky Derby.

For old-time Appalachian speakers, however, *poor-do* possessed a fluid meaning that evidently covered a number of homely prepara-tions of similar texture and consistency. Essentially, they were gruels bulked out with meat, as a very similar Rhineland poverty food *Wurst-brei* (pudding mush) implies. If the Pennsylvania Germans brought scrapple to Appalachia, it did not survive the harsh conditions of the mountains. Poor-do and burgoo, the gentrified stew that has now evolved out of it, derived in concept from poverty foods of the British Isles. But of one thing we can be certain: When the Appalachian set-tlers in poor-do country killed a hog and made scrapple, they proba-bly ate it as hot mush in true medieval fashion. As one recent Tennessee informant put it, "We don't linger over poor-do; we want to get at it directly."[61]

Pashofa: The South's First Pork Scrapple

Poor-do country happens to straddle the old heartland of the Chero-kee Nation, and while it is tempting to look for similar dishes in Cherokee cookery—and there are several—the historical reality is that the Europeans who settled in North America did not view Native American food preparation with high esteem. It was not something they wanted to imitate. While European settlers were quite taken with many native plant foods, they invariably adapted them to European cooking methods and to European ideas about acceptable color, taste, and texture.

On the other hand, there were a number of Native American peo-ples who prepared dishes similar to scrapple long before Europeans arrived on this continent. Centuries earlier they had devised various combinations of meat and cornmeal (or acorn mush) to make stews and gruels that met their dietary and ritual needs. Foods introduced by the Europeans greatly altered these traditional preparations, espe-cially with the introduction of domesticated animals like the hog. One of the most interesting of these altered foods is Chickasaw and Choctaw *pashofa*, which has employed pork as its major meat ingre-dient for several hundred years. It is one of the Native American dishes that come closest to scrapple, and it deserves a place in southern cooking that is almost always overlooked by food historians.

The date when *pashofa* intersected with pigs is well documented. In 1541, Spanish explorer Hernando DeSoto and an army of some seven hundred men, plus hundreds of horses, pigs, and other livestock, traveled north from Florida into Mississippi. When they came into contact with the Chickasaw, the Spaniards treated them brutally, and this resulted in retaliatory Chickasaw raids. The Chickasaw managed to make off with large amounts of weapons and hundreds of pigs and horses, and from that time on, *pashofa* and hogs appear to have evolved together in the cookery of these people. It is certainly no exaggeration to give the Chickasaw credit as the South's first hog farmers, because once they acquired the pigs, they valued them highly.

Pashofa is a stew made with fresh pork and cracked white flint corn somewhat coarser in texture than commercial small hominy. The cornmeal was traditionally prepared in a gum (a hollowed-out stump) or in a large section of log converted into a mortar known as a hominy block. As the kernels were beaten, the husks were blown away by means of reed fans until the meal achieved a consistent texture. It was then placed in large pots with water and wood ash or salt, and boiled for hours until slightly undercooked. The corn was then removed from the pot, dried, and pounded together with an equal quantity of fresh meat chopped very fine (today this is almost always pork). The meat and corn mixture was then returned to the cooking vessel and boiled until thick. In earlier times, the gruel was generally served cold in wooden bowls or horn spoons. At the Pashofa Dance, during which participants hoped to drive out Shulop, the Spirit of Disease, from a tribal member who was sick, *pashofa*

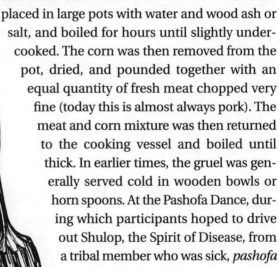

Hominy block and pestle for crushing pashofa *corn.*

Traditional Pashofa Cookpots

Chickasaw potter Joanna Underwood has taken a special interest in reviving the traditional raku-fired vessels of the ancient Mississippian peoples. Her handsome pottery, including *pashofa* cookpots, may be viewed on the website of the Chickasaw Nation centered at Ada, Oklahoma. For information, go to www.chickasaw.net and click on culture and art.

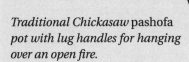

Traditional Chickasaw pashofa *pot with lug handles for hanging over an open fire.*

was served hot to all those involved in the healing ceremony. Since *pashofa* could be kept for as long as a month during cold weather, it was also common in some households to slice it and reheat it in a frying pan like traditional scrapple.

The concept behind *pashofa* probably dates to the time of the ancient mound builders in the Mississippi River Valley. Today it is made by the mound builders' presumed descendants, the Choctaw and Chickasaw, who originally formed one tribe. In the 1830s, President Andrew Jackson decided to clean out the native peoples living in the South and force them to move west to what is now Oklahoma. But up to that time, these cultures were very much a part of the culinary synthesis taking place in many parts of the Deep South, especially since they were also slaveowners and often intermarried with blacks. The symbolic role that *pashofa* plays in Chickasaw and Choctaw society is perhaps best underlined by the care that is taken in growing the special variety of corn used for making the dish. It is still planted by both tribes in Oklahoma. Around 1900, Charles Tucker, a Mississippi Chickasaw, brought the *pashofa* corn back to old Chickasaw country around Iuka, Mississippi, in the belief that once it grew again on ancestral soil, the Chickasaw would be able to come home.

New Wave Scrapple and the "Scrappledelphia Sound"

If the Civil War gave birth to commercial slaughterhouse scrapple, World War II gave birth to a countercurrent that is with us even to this day: the rise in beef consumption. During the early 1950s, beef consumption in the United States soon outpaced that of pork, which had been the most widely consumed meat since the colonial period.[62] The reasons are many: industrialization of feed lots, post–World War II affluence, and especially suburbanization, the so-called California lifestyle, and a shift to grilled foods on the patio. Call it the victory of the hamburger. As beef became the new status meat of the station wagon set, pork declined in popularity and became more and more associated with poverty foods, small-town eating habits, and the "down home" cooking of the black South. This was a period when food assumed strange new nuances under the social stresses of desegregation, the flight of ethnic communities to the suburbs, the advent of TV, and squeaky-clean, red-white-and-blue innocence. This was not an era of grand accomplishments in American cookery, even though tuna fish casserole is probably here to stay. In this new milieu, it became trendy to deride regional pork dishes like scrapple, and this mantra is still repeated over and over in the food media; all the while, almost 40 percent of America has gotten grossly obese on junk food and sugar.

Grits and hominy disappeared from Philadelphia menus in the 1890s due to the same kind of cultural rejection. In fact, all over the country, regional foods slipped away into the shadows of history because they were associated with an America that was different from the one we know today and, unfortunately, were depicted by some patriotic societies as much too exclusively their own. Philadelphia scrapple was fortunate in that it was also *Panhas*. The Pennsylvania Dutch farmers who supply the city with its produce and meats change their ways at their own pace, so scrapple survived into the food revival of the 1970s. In spite of the hard-hitting lyrics of Robin Remailly's acid-folk song "Happy Scrapple Daddy," which appeared in 1971 on his classic album *Good Taste Is Timeless*, the real carnage was not in the slaughterhouses but in Vietnam.

Evan Jones discussed scrapple in *American Food*, but the recipe he included was not a traditional one, if we may characterize traditional as the sort of dish prepared in the early 1800s by Elizabeth Ellicott Lea or Elizabeth Nicholson.[63] Jones's recipe was made with sausage, obviously a convenience for his readers, but also silent testimony to the fact that American scrapple might be headed in a new direction. It took about twenty years for the food and dining revolution in the United States to take root in the far reaches of the country. Yes, indeed, Alice Waters rediscovered regional cookery at Chez Panisse in Berkeley, a hippie experiment turned trendsetter if ever there was one.[64] Now regional cooks are also rediscovering themselves and the foods around them. Since *scrapple* is an American word with very localized American meanings, New Wave cookery—that uptown take on *goût du terroir*—has grabbed the idea and run with it.

In Boston, we find salmon scrapple garnished with sea urchin roe and lobster scrapple drizzled with a citrus-saffron emulsion. In New York, there is scrapple of arctic char spiced with *piment d'Espellette* (a pepper from the Basque region of France), served in a puddle of fig glaze. In Chicago, black bean scrapple surfaces on high-tech Mexican menus, and if the salsa is served straight from a stone mortar, the gods of the Aztecs will surely visit you in your dreams. In Houston, it's emu scrapple with manchemantel sauce (about sixteen ingredients) and jicama coleslaw. In Los Angeles, where food standing on end is all the rage, wild boar scrapple with ancho chiles and rosemary gremolata defies gravity until probed by an exploring fork. Money may buy a seat at these restaurants, but is this scrapple rooted to the true spirit of the dish any more than the leaping dolphins of frozen Victorian Nesselrode came from the sea? Jaded Romans ate flamingo tongues because they had lost touch with real food and nature.

Elvis Presley never crooned a love song to scrapple, but during his sojourns in Philadelphia, there were scrapple advertisements on the local radio that featured an orchestra of singing canaries. Canaries have the remarkable ability to warn us when the air is going bad, and something tells me the aroma of scrapple has changed. New Wave scrapple is indeed quirky, and probably so gilded and rarefied in its cultural transfusions that it could only be worthy of adorning the covers of *Food Arts*. Like so much of American cooking today, the cacophony of tricks and textures reflects a real collapse of what the Romans called *sensus communis,* a shared system of categorizing and ordering society. There is no common identity. American cookery is in a state of civil war.

The man who kept the soul in scrapple was Charlie "Bird" Parker (1920–55), the saxophonist whose nimble fingers gave us the bebop

Scrapple Aloha.

classic "Scrapple from the Apple." Charlie Parker knew all about scrapple, but his was Harlem scrapple transformed into music, a fitting nod to the scrabblin' mush of his forefathers as well as to the buckwheat meadows that once flourished on that part of old Manhattan. Because of him, scrapple of another kind is now known all over the world. It is scrapple with a universal voice, and that is what is meant by the Scrappledelphia Sound, a term I did not invent, by the way.

You can hear it in the hum of Philadelphia's Italian Market, in the splash of the shad making their way up the Delaware each spring. It is the silence of a Quaker meeting, and the tolling of the bells of Saints Peter and Paul Cathedral on Logan Circle. It is the snappy crunch of fresh pretzels and the soft-shoe tap dance of an old man on South Street. It is the clang of trollies, the strum of mummers, and the sound of plates set down on a common table, where the whole city sits down together to feast.

You do not need to live in Philadelphia to hear this music. Cut yourself a slice of real scrapple, and while you brown it in the skillet, take a slice of canned pineapple (as the recipe directs), and caramelize it in a small skillet to one side. Turn on Charlie Parker's "Scrapple from the Apple," and pour yourself a glass of Hawaiian Punch with a splash of bourbon (use Coke if you are southern). Put the glazed pineapple on top of the scrapple in a dish of an appropriately bright color. Stick a small parasol in the pineapple to give the meal a festive appearance, and take your scrapple to the terrace, jiving as you go in your best set of shades. A little sip of punch, a little more volume to Charlie Parker. Yes, this is Americana, and the dish is called Scrapple Aloha.

Some Scrapple Recipes for Home Cooking

Making scrapple at home not only can be fun as a family project, but also is one way to control the sort of ingredients that go into your food. The recipes in this chapter demonstrate the wide range of possibilities available to home scrapple makers, from a traditional Wisconsin Amish recipe to a totally vegan wild rice and mushroom scrapple, which, by the way, really does taste like Philadelphia scrapple. There are also a lot of scrapples that are interesting from a historical standpoint but are not included here because of their highly specialized appeal. Among these are the unusual fresh scrapples or "soup" scrapples, which hark back to medieval gruels and are often served over boiled potatoes or hash browns. Until recently, you could actually order soup scrapple, eaten with a spoon, at the Red Byrd Restaurant on Route 34 in Keedysville, Maryland. The Red Byrd, now out of business, was a local eatery described by the *Washington Post* as "crummy but good"; its slippery pot pies were a local legend.

The legendary quality of good Pennsylvania Dutch home cooking was one of the great enthusiasms of Bland Johaneson's *Victualary among the Pennsylvania Germans,* a small booklet published in 1928 by the Society of Pennsylvania German Gastronomes.[65] There was indeed such an association of traditional cooks who prided themselves on their culinary craftsmanship, but those days passed many years ago. Johaneson rightly singled out scrapple as a food that, in spite of its simplicity, requires a certain amount of good technique to get it right. His comments had a lasting influence, firing the imagination of a long line of Pennsylvania Dutch cookbook writers beginning with J. George Frederick, whose *Pennsylvania Dutch and Their Cookery* was published in 1935. On the other hand, none of these authors, Johaneson included, looked at scrapple as anything other than *Panhas*. The history, like the art of cooking scrapple, is much more complex.

Utensils for Scrapple Making

Before trying the recipes, familiarize yourself with the utensils you need to prepare and cook scrapple with the least amount of inconvenience. Here is a list of what you should have on hand before you start:

- A stainless steel 4-quart (4-liter) stewing pan, preferably heavy cast. A thin metal bottom will allow the scrapple to scorch while it is cooking.

- A sharp stainless steel knife for cutting meat into stewing-size pieces.

- A nonreactive work bowl, such as stainless steel or glass. This is called for in recipes where acids might otherwise interact with the container. Not all types of plastic are safe. In fact, research is beginning to show that most plastics are not as stable as previously assumed.

- Kitchen scales. The recipes can be made without a set of scales, but for greater accuracy and less waste of food, it is worth the investment. The scales need not be expensive.

- A cutting board or clean cutting surface, preferably wood. Plastic cutting surfaces have been shown to retain more microbes than wood and are harder to sterilize.

- A meat grinder or food processor that will process meat to various textures. Nearly all of the recipes were tested several times with an Enterprise meat grinder and with a large, professional model Cuisinart food processor.

- A stirring paddle. I use one with a large hole in the paddle end so that the scrapple can pass through it while stirring. This helps create a better texture.

- A sifter for flour and cornmeal.

- A reliable timer. If you lack a timer on your stove, use the one on your microwave oven. The recipes presented here have been timed carefully, so it is advisable to time yourself when you start. This will help you better calculate your own cooking pace once you master scrapple making.

- Bread pans. I use large pans, roughly 5$\frac{1}{2}$ inches wide by 10$\frac{1}{2}$ inches long, as shown in the drawing below. Each pan yields a loaf of scrapple weighing about 5 pounds (2$\frac{1}{2}$ kg). The same amount of scrapple also fits into small sets of bread pans that are sold soldered together (see below). Since there are so many different sizes of bread pans, I have approximated the total number of servings. Have at least four large bread pans on hand in case you need them. Once you have made a batch of scrapple, you will be able to judge how many portions you can get in each of your pans. Your bread pans for scrapple making should be metal. Scrapple cools more slowly in glass pans and becomes watery. This moisture is sweated off the surface of the scrapple and causes it to be soft and difficult to slice.

- A large, heavy, cast-iron skillet for frying scrapple. Use a splatter screen over the skillet while the scrapple is cooking. The recipes below are generally low-fat, but particles of oats, corn, or rice in the various recipes sometimes pop and may burn someone standing nearby, especially a small child.

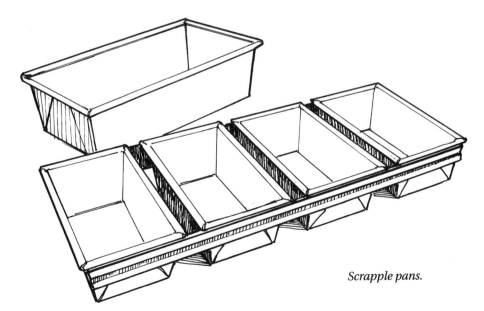

Scrapple pans.

Taste and Texture

Are there differences between homemade scrapple and commercial scrapple? The answer is yes. The differences are many—so many, in fact, that it is best to think of your homemade scrapple as a totally different food product. Yet with some experimentation, it is possible on a stovetop to create homemade scrapples that imitate some of the better features of those made by professional butchers. Flavor and texture are two important factors.

As a rule of thumb, the best traditional butchers are the ones who also raise their own animals, or commission a local farmer to do it for them, and slaughter in small quantities. Small family butchers usually practice "hot meat," or "hot bone," processing. This means that they begin to process the animal into sausage, scrapple, and other products as soon as it is killed. Large, commercial meat packers, which process hundreds of animals at a time, cannot make meat products this way since they must refrigerate the carcasses for the next stage of processing. The fresher the meat, the better the flavor. Small firms like Dietrich's Meats in Krumsville, Pennsylvania, Mack's Liver Mush in Shelby, North Carolina, and Ratchford's in Guyton, Georgia, have captured niche markets with high-quality food products because of their small scale. When buying ingredients for your own scrapple, you can help traditional butchers and save family farms by purchasing locally raised meats.

Many cooks and restaurants are now taking this one step farther by demanding to know how the animals were raised. There is a strong movement toward supporting free-range pigs, not only because the meat has a better flavor, but also because the animals were not raised and killed under stress. Pigs are curious and extremely intelligent, much like dogs in some ways, and they can figure out quickly what is in store for them at the slaughterhouse. Pigs have been our faithful servants for several thousand years. It does behoove us to treat them—and all animals—with dignity, and not view their lives as something to be wasted.

It is often thought that waste products are the only things that end up in scrapple, but this is not necessarily the case. A quick look at the recipes in this chapter will not reveal anything too unusual or offbeat. The truth is that more odds and ends go into commercial scrapples than into the small artisanal products made by most of the producers listed at the back of this book. Far worse things end up in many processed beef products, such as hot dogs and fast-food hamburgers, and especially in commercial pepperonis, so it is hypocritical to criticize one and not the other. Some of the tasters who tested my scrapple recipes actually missed the "grease and heartburn." This was a surprising criticism. In response to that, I can only say that when one has grown accustomed to eating inferior grades of scrapple, the delicate recipes with low fat will of course lack something to a palate used to fatty tastes. Fat is a great transmitter of flavor, and some commercial brands of scrapple rely on it to make up for other deficiencies.

One of the deficiencies is the meal used for thickening scrapple. This in turn relates to texture and crust. Most scrapple makers do not think of scrapple as a porridge or gruel, or judge its flavor by the batter before it is poured into pans. Good-quality cornmeal makes all the difference, and so much the better when it is stone-ground. There are also recipes that call for self-rising cornmeal. This is nonsense and probably unhealthful. This type of cornmeal contains chemical leavenings, which add unnecessary chemical salts to the food and do nothing to improve the scrapple. Why should scrapple rise up like bread?

The secret to a good texture in scrapple lies in the cooking. Verna Dietrich of Dietrich's Meats told me that she cooks her scrapple for 5 hours, and most of the other firms do likewise, even for liver mush. Long, slow cooking breaks down the starches in the flours as well as the particles of meat. Constant stirring makes the batter creamier, thicker, and lighter because air is being stirred into it. This will result in a firm loaf and a slice of scrapple that fries nicely. All of the recipes below provide stirring times; a strong arm will not replace impatience. Just keep stirring, and stir the scrapple more than you think necessary. It is impossible to stir scrapple too much, but you know it is ready when it pulls away from the pan and resembles mashed potatoes. An accomplished scrapple cook knows this by the feel of the pot stick, but anyone can learn by trial and error.

How to Cook and Serve Scrapple

Scrapple is easy to cook, but there is a technique to it. Lightly grease a heavy skillet, then heat it over a high flame. Once the skillet is very hot, reduce the heat to low and add the scrapple. Let the scrapple brown on one side (about 8 to 10 minutes), then flip it over and brown the other. Too much flipping will ruin it, but the old adage that you cook scrapple only once on each side is not at all a firm rule. Different scrapples cook differently, and not all skillets transmit heat the same way. Once there is golden crust on each side, the scrapple is ready to serve. It should be served immediately while it is hot; cold scrapple is just as unappealing as a cold omelet.

What do you do with the scrapple you haven't yet fried? It will keep in the refrigerator for a week or two, and some scrapples actually improve in flavor when they are a day or two old. But since the refrigerator is constantly being opened and closed, there is no guarantee that it will maintain your scrapple at a constant temperature. Sooner or later the scrapple may begin to spoil, especially if it contains rice, beans, corn, or mushrooms.

This brings me to the hotly debated issue of freezing scrapple. This is recommended in many recipes, but it is a certain way to ruin scrapple. Freezing scrapple causes the water particles to crystallize and separate. When it is thawed, the water runs out, and the scrapple turns to mush. If there is no other alternative, however, it is possible to freeze scrapple and avoid some of the worst problems. This can be accomplished by slicing the scrapple and dusting each piece very lightly with flour. Then individually wrap each slice in plastic wrap and freeze in air-tight freezer bags. Thaw the slices on paper towels or some other absorbent surface, then dust again with a little flour or cornmeal. This should avoid the worst of the mushiness.

Freezing also does something to the flavor of the scrapple. The taste of herbs fades, a bitterness in pork liver can be amplified, venison scrapple seems to get gamier, and cornmeal can taste stale. Complex chemical reactions are probably taking place while the scrapple is frozen—enzyme breakdowns and the like. None of this has been well studied, but it only goes to prove that scrapple is best consumed shortly after it is made—as true today as it was in the Middle Ages.

Scrapple and Nutrition

Another gray area is the nutritional role of scrapple. Food journalists looking for hot topics often have heaped criticism on scrapple without really knowing much about it or its role in everyday diet. The *Bal-*

timore Citypaper ran an article in 2000 based on some heavily skewed nutritional data supplied by the University of Maryland.[66] The target was Baltimore's penchant for such regional foods and drinks as scrapple, rye whiskey, fried oysters, and the like. The problem with the data was that each food was taken out of context; how it fits into the total dietary picture is far more important than whether a particular food has a high fat content. A shot of rye whiskey prior to breakfast was an old-time custom done to help the digestion of scrapple much the same way that Russians take vodka before eating fat-rich caviar. Baltimore scrapple should have been compared with a slice of Brie or a country pâté (its close French relative). The real issue is that scrapple cannot be condemned on the basis of one or two brands alone, because every firm makes a different product. There are simply too many variables at play.

In any case, scrapple needs no apology. Many nutritionists are now coming to realize that fat is not the culprit, and many scrapples are much lower in fat than most people suspect. Furthermore, scrapples are rich in protein, so they can be formulated to make an appealing, low-cost food that takes into account regional eating preferences. Liver mush is very high in protein and has about 8 percent fat in a 2-ounce slice. Since it is much healthier than most junk foods, liver mush is undergoing a revival in North Carolina. In addition, ethnographers have shown that in areas where there was high consumption of liver mush, liver pudding, and other pork liver products, there was a much lower incidence of pellagra. And the Appalachian hill folk who lived on greens and poor-do rarely died of obesity. What is lacking are good studies of the role of traditional foods like scrapple in rural diets, what made them work, and what adjustments, if any, need to be made for an urban lifestyle. In the meantime, one thing is clear: Eating scrapple in conjunction with a pickle such as scrapple sauce is much healthier than simply eating it alone or with syrup. Vinegar helps block the uptake of bad fats in the body, and this is probably one reason why old-time farmers could eat scrapple with gusto into their nineties. For this reason, I have also included a few relish recipes for serving with scrapple. The recipes are organized in alphabetical order. Yields are approximate. Recipes can be halved or doubled without making alterations in the ingredients.

1. Apple Relish for Scrapple

This easy-to-make relish can be prepared at the last minute. It is best eaten the day it is made, although it will keep a few days in the refrigerator.

YIELD: 2 cups (450 g)

1/2 cup (75 g) finely chopped onion
1 tablespoon (15 ml) oil, preferably olive oil
1 cup (200 g) pickled watermelon rind cut into tiny dice
3 cups (375 g) diced tart apple, such as Granny Smith
2 teaspoons minced fresh rosemary
salt to taste

Put the onion and oil in a saucepan and cover. Cook gently over medium heat until the onion begins to soften and turn yellow, about 4 minutes. Add the diced watermelon, apple, and rosemary. Stir to combine the ingredients thoroughly, then cover and continue cooking until the mixture is hot, about 8 minutes; do not overcook the apples. Remove from heat, add salt to taste, and serve as a condiment with fried scrapple.

2. Buffalo Scrapple (Wheeler County, Texas)

Emmanuel Dubbs, a buffalo hunter from Stark County, Ohio, described his life on the lower Great Plains during the 1870s. The last of the great buffalo herds were being rounded up and shot for their tongues, considered a delicacy, and for their hides, which sold at the time for $2.00 or $2.50 each. Dubbs saw the discarded carcasses as a financial opportunity and marketed sugar-cured buffalo, processed like sugar-cured hams, to dealers in Kansas City. He never said whether he made buffalo scrapple (his neighbors did), but he traveled with ample supplies of cornmeal, and most significantly, he remarked, "We only had an old broken spade that we used about our camp fire in cooking."[67] Thus he had the meat, the cornmeal, and the griddle. Dubbs eventually settled on a farm in Wheeler County, Texas.

Samuel Arnold, owner of the Fort Restaurant up on the side of the Rockies overlooking Denver, offered some helpful advice in getting this recipe to come together. His book *Eating Up the Santa Fe Trail* is a useful guide to food habits in the Old West. It was Sam's idea to add jalapeño peppers (a nice touch—try it), but Texas bird peppers probably would have been Dubbs's local choice if he liked spicy food. Otherwise, the addition of buffaloberries—if you can get them—would give it an authentic Great Plains nuance. This recipe is a collage of cultures, with emphasis on the Mexican side of the Texas table. It also can be used as stuffing in tamales.

YIELD: 18 to 20 servings

2 pounds (1 kg) buffalo meat (frozen ground patties are ideal)
juice of 1½ limes
1 cup (150 g) chopped onion
1 tablespoon minced garlic
1 tablespoon salt
½ teaspoon coarsely ground bird peppers (or any hot red
    pepper to taste)
1 tablespoon ground coriander
1½ teaspoons ground nutmeg
3 to 4 cups (465 to 625 g) yellow cornmeal

Obtaining Buffalo Meat and Buffaloberries

Buffalo meat is not easy to find in some parts of the country. The very best quality organically raised meat can be ordered over the Internet at www.greatrangebison.com, the website of Rocky Mountain Natural Meats, 6911 Washington St., Denver, CO 80229-6702, telephone (800) 327-2706. Eastern-raised buffalo of the same high quality can be obtained from Georgetown Farm, P.O. Box 558, Madison, VA 22727, telephone (888) FAT-LEAN, website www.eatlean.com. My recipe was tested with meat from Georgetown Farm.

Buffaloberries *(Shepherdia argentea)* are among the most handsome of the Great Plains shrubs, covered as they are with distinctive narrow, silvery gray leaves and, in the autumn, with bright red fruits. Native peoples gathered these fruits and ate them raw or dried for winter use. As their name implies, the berries were used in conjunction with buffalo in the same way as cranberry sauce with turkey. They are delightful when added to buffalo scrapple, but of course, you must live on the Great Plains to find them. Today most people make jelly with the berries, but this greatly underestimates their culinary potential.

Texas bird peppers.

If the meat is whole, cut it up into irregular ice-cube-size pieces. Put the chunks or ground patties in a nonreactive bowl, and squeeze the fresh lime juice over it. Marinate 30 to 40 minutes, then pour off all excess liquid. Do not rinse the meat.

Bring 2 1/2 quarts (2 1/2 liters) of water to boil in a heavy 3- to 4-quart (3- to 4-liter) stewing pot. Add the meat, onion, garlic, salt, and hot pepper. Boil gently over medium heat 40 minutes, skimming off any scum that rises to the surface. Strain out the meat and onion mixture, and return the stock to the pot. Chop or grind the meat and onion to an even consistency, and return to the cooking stock. Add the coriander and nutmeg, and gradually sift in the cornmeal, alternating between sifting and stirring to avoid lumps. Then stir vigorously so that the mixture thickens and becomes ropy (about 15 to 20 minutes). Once the scrapple thickens, pour it into a lightly greased bread pan, filling to the top. Set on a rack to cool, then refrigerate overnight. The next day, slice and brown in a skillet lightly brushed with oil.

3. Clam Scrapple (Cape May, New Jersey)

Scrapple purists may gasp at the many strange mutations that scrapple has undergone since the 1950s, but in fact, this shellfish variation on the scrapple concept dates to the 1890s at least. It may have evolved out of leftover puree of clams as conceived by Helen Louise Johnson for one of her Enterprise meat grinder recipes, and it is not too remote in structure from the cornmeal-and-fish mush dishes once made by the local Lenape peoples prior to European settlement. The basic premise of old-fashioned clam scrapple, however, was health: a light summer alternative to meat, yet structurally similar to the grits scrapples popular in parts of Ohio, southern Indiana, and Illinois. In Missouri, a type of catfish scrapple is still made in some of the Mississippi River towns, using catfish and fish stock where this

New Jersey recipe uses clams. Incidentally, clam scrapple gave birth to yet another variant: oyster scrapple made with shredded wheat (the commercial cereal) instead of grits.

YIELD: 25 to 30 servings

4 1/2 cups (1 1/8 liters) water
4 1/2 cups (1 1/8 liters) clam juice
1 tablespoon salt
1 pound (500 g) chopped cooked clams
   (canned clams may be used)
1/2 pound (250 g) shredded crabmeat
1 cup (150 g) chopped onion
1 teaspoon dried thyme
1 teaspoon ground mace
1/2 teaspoon ground white pepper
2 cups (300 g) old-fashioned white grits
1 cup (155 g) white cornmeal

Combine the water, clam juice, salt, clams, crab, and onion in a large stewing pan. Bring to a boil over medium-high heat, then reduce to a simmer for 15 minutes. Strain and return the broth to the pan. Grind the clam mixture until reduced to a fine, even texture. Return

"Down the shore" at Atlantic City, New Jersey, 1910.
ROUGHWOOD COLLECTION

this to the broth, and bring to a gentle boil over a medium heat. Add the thyme, mace, pepper, grits, and cornmeal and cook until thick (about 25 minutes). Stir often so that the scrapple breaks down to a smooth, creamy texture. Once it is thick and ropy, pour into lightly greased bread pans and refrigerate overnight. The next day, turn out of the pans, slice into 1/2-inch (1-cm) thick slices, dust with flour or fine breadcrumbs, and brown in a lightly greased skillet.

4. "Goetta" Oatmeal Scrapple (Woodville, Ohio)

I was given this recipe many years ago by Marian Sheffer Buehler (1901–80), an Ohio-born poet who lived at Sprucemont, a 1767 farmhouse in Devon, Pennsylvania. Marian was one of the founding members of "Poets Walk In," a group that included such luminaries as Mary Hoxie Jones and Elizabeth Gray Vining. But it wasn't her poetry that captivated my attention; it was Marian's love for the old German settlement around Woodville, Ohio, where she was born. The attic of Sprucemont was cram-packed with wooden shoes, spinning wheels, and other museum-quality heirlooms from Woodville's nineteenth-century German community. Marian also spoke Oldenburger Platt, probably one of the last of her generation who could actually tell stories (and write poems) in that dialect. All that is gone now, but Marian's recipe lives on as a reminder that northern Ohio's culinary history is a rich mix of Old World and New.

One of the most interesting Old World features of Marian's recipe is the use of dried fruit. Its addition to goetta is an idea tracing to the Middle Ages and forms a culinary bridge between meat gruels and the plum puddings or mincemeats of English tradition. The introduction of dried fruit was not limited to goetta; it was a common practice in many affluent north German households, especially for festive occasions. In Westphalia, *Panhas* prepared with dried fruit was known as *Möppkenbrot*, an old word that implied a finer type of food, something akin to fruitcake.

Because steel-cut oatmeal requires long cooking, the goetta will be somewhat soupy when the oatmeal is first added, but it will cook down to the proper consistency in an hour, provided it is stirred often. Do not use rolled oats for making goetta; they will dissolve into a paste.

YIELD: 25 to 30 servings

3 cups (450 g) steel-cut oatmeal
1 pound (500 g) beef, such as stewing beef, cut into cubes

1 pound (500 g) pork cut into cubes, or 1/2 pound (250 g) pork
   heart plus 1/2 pound (250 g) ground pork sausage
1 tablespoon salt
1 tablespoon ground summer savory
1 teaspoon ground marjoram
2 teaspoons black pepper
11/2 cups (150 g) Zanté currants

Put the oatmeal in a deep bowl and cover with 1 quart (1 liter) boiling water. Set aside to soften while the meat is cooking. Add more boiling water if the oatmeal absorbs all the liquid. Put the meat in a deep stewing pan with 21/2 quarts (21/2 liters) of water, and cook over medium-high heat for 1 hour. Strain the meat from the stock, and return the stock to the pan. Grind half the meat to a fine paste consistency, and grind the other half to a loose, coarse texture. Add the ground meat to the stock. Drain any excess liquid from the oatmeal, and add the oatmeal to the stock. Bring the goetta to a gentle boil over medium heat and cook, stirring often to create a thick, creamy consistency. After 30 minutes, add the seasonings. Continue cooking until the mixture is thick, about another 30 minutes. When it is ready to remove from the stove, stir in the currants, then pour the goetta into pans to cool. After it has cooled, cover and refrigerate. The next day, remove from the pans, slice and fry like scrapple, or serve at room temperature like a meat pâté.

5. Ham Scrapple (Mount Holly Springs, Pennsylvania)

"My mother would take the bone of a baked ham and boil it in water until the meat could be scraped off easily. Then she boiled cornmeal in the stock and added the ham. It made a scrapple with very special flavor. Another thing she would do was heat up pot pudding until it was thick like gravy, then pour it pretty heavy over corn flapjacks. That made a meal in itself." These are the words of retired dentist L. Wilbur Zimmerman, recollecting his Mennonite childhood at Mount Holly Springs during the early 1900s. The secret to flavorful old-time ham scrapple is the ham, so choose it carefully. It is better to use a hickory-smoked ham, such as Smithfield's or Dietrich's picnic ham, because the commercial, water-packed hams sold in most supermarkets today lack sufficient flavor to give the scrapple "that special something" the dish requires. Serve it the Mount Holly Springs way, with a side dish of stewed peaches.

YIELD: 18 to 20 servings

1¹/2 pounds (750 g) well-flavored country ham, outer rind
    removed
³/4 cup (125 g) hickory-smoked bacon, coarsely chopped
1 cup (175 g) country ham cut into tiny dice
1 teaspoon salt
2 teaspoons coarsely grated black pepper
1 tablespoon ground sage
1 tablespoon ground savory
¹/4 teaspoon ground cloves
3 cups (465 g) yellow cornmeal

Bring 2¹/2 quarts (2¹/2 liters) of water to a boil in a heavy 3- to 4-
quart (3- to 4-liter) stewing pan. Cut the ham into large, irregular
pieces, and add to the water along with the chopped bacon. Boil gently over medium heat for 40 minutes, skimming off any fat that rises

Weaverland Ham Stock

A distinctive ham-and-onion taste is something many Pennsylvania Dutch cooks look for in their everyday recipes. For an alternate way to make the stock for Wilbur Zimmerman's childhood
dish, use ham hocks or an equivalent amount of meaty ham
bones. This recipe comes from Weaverland in eastern Lancaster
County, Pennsylvania.

YIELD: 2 quarts (2 liters)

1 large ham hock, about 1¹/2 pounds (750 g)
2 small turnips, pared and quartered
1 carrot, pared and cut into 3 pieces
¹/2 onion (about 150 g), quartered
3 fresh bay leaves (optional)
¹/2 cup (50 g) chopped celery leaves

Put all the ingredients into a deep stewing pan with 3 quarts (3
liters) of water, and simmer over medium heat for 2 hours, or
until reduced to 2 quarts (2 liters). Skim off any scum that may
form while the stock is cooking. Once the stock is reduced, strain,
discard the vegetables, and use the stock and meat for making
Ham Scrapple.

Recipe pamphlet, circa 1930.
ROUGHWOOD COLLECTION

to the surface. Strain out the meat, and return the stock to the stewing pan. Chop or grind the ham and bacon to a fine consistency, and add to the cooking stock, along with the diced ham and seasonings. Gradually sift in the cornmeal, alternating between sifting and stirring to avoid lumps. Then stir vigorously so that the mixture thickens and becomes ropy (about 15 to 20 minutes). Once the scrapple thickens, pour it into a lightly greased bread pan, filling to the top. Set on a rack to cool, then refrigerate overnight. The next day, slice and brown in a skillet lightly brushed with oil.

6. Hoopes's Scrapple Sauce

My grandmother obtained this recipe from Margaret Hoopes, an acquaintance of her mother's who used to attend Marlborough Friends Meeting near Unionville, Chester County, Pennsylvania, in the 1930s. The recipe came from the family of scrapple maker Percy Hoopes, who used to sell the sauce in old-style pickle jars. The secret to its flavor is simple: Scrapple has sage in it, thus a little sage in the sauce enhances the taste of both.

YIELD: 6 pints (1 1/2 liters)

4 quarts (6 pounds/3 kg) green tomatoes chopped to a coarse puree
2 cups (300 g) onion, chopped to a coarse puree

1/4 cup (60 g) sea salt or pickling salt

2 cups (500 g) sugar

3 tablespoons hot chili pepper, chopped fine (or quantity to taste)

3 cups (750 ml) apple cider vinegar

1 tablespoon white mustard seed

2 teaspoons celery seed

2 tablespoons freshly grated ginger root

1/3 cup (25 g) finely minced fresh sage leaves, or 2 tablespoons
  ground dry sage leaves

1 cup (125 g) sweet red pepper cut into tiny dice

Put the tomatoes, onion, salt, sugar, hot pepper, vinegar, mustard, and celery seed in a deep preserving pan, and cook steadily over medium-high heat for 30 minutes, or until the liquid part is reduced by one-fourth and the sauce is thick. Then add the ginger, sage, and sweet pepper. Continue cooking for 10 to 15 minutes, then pour the sauce into hot, sanitized jars and seal. This sauce will keep for more than a year.

7. Kickapoo Valley *Panhas* (Wisconsin)

The Amish community in Wisconsin has given us many remarkable foods, one of the best known being the Amish paste tomato, an heirloom variety that is now grown all over the United States. But the Amish have also taken many traditional dishes west from their old home in Pennsylvania, and this traditional-style *Panhas* is one of them. The flavor of this recipe is very close to the old-fashioned scrapples made by Elizabeth Nicholson and Elizabeth Ellicott Lea, except that many Amish like to eat scrapple with liver pudding as gravy. Such high-protein fare is well suited to their vigorous lifestyle on the farm. With a cup of steaming hot coffee and a slice of shoofly pie to top it off, who needs lunch?

YIELD: 25 to 30 servings

1 pound (500 g) pork liver

1 pound (500 g) pork heart

1/2 pound (250 g) pork trimmings or unseasoned
  freshly ground pork sausage

1 tablespoon salt

1 1/2 tablespoons ground sage

1 teaspoon black pepper
1 teaspoon ground mace
1/4 teaspoon ground cloves
3 cups (465 g) cornmeal
1 cup (125 g) buckwheat flour

Cut the liver and heart into small pieces for stewing. Add this and the rest of the meat to 2 1/2 quarts (2 1/2 liters) of boiling water in a large, 4-quart (4-liter) stewing pan. Stew over medium heat for 1 hour, skimming off any fat that rises to the surface. Strain out the meat, and return the stock to the pan. Grind half the meat to a fine paste and the other half to a coarse consistency. Add the ground meat to the stock, then add the seasonings. Combine the cornmeal and buckwheat flour, and gradually sift this into the stock, whisking and stirring as you add the meal. Stir over medium heat for 25 to 30 minutes, or until the scrapple becomes thick and ropy. Pour into lightly greased pans and cool. Once cool, refrigerate overnight, then turn out of the pans, slice, and fry.

8. Pennsylvania Dutch *Metzelsupp*

I first published this recipe in *Pennsylvania Dutch Country Cooking*. It was based on an interview with an old country butcher from Germantown in Snyder County, Pennsylvania. My recipe is considerably simplified from the long, arduous process of butchering and making the white stock outdoors in a large iron kettle. The stovetop version takes about 25 minutes to prepare. The rich, flavorful stock requires about 2 hours. This is an excellent soup as a first course or a cold-weather main dish. The mix and choice of sausages are really a matter of personal taste.

YIELD: 8 to 10 servings

3 quarts (3 liters) pork stock
6 ounces (180 g) liver sausage, skinned and chopped
1 teaspoon ground summer savory
1 teaspoon ground sage
4 ounces (125 g) coriander-flavored smoked sausage, sliced
4 ounces (125 g) veal sausage, sliced lengthwise, then cut into
    diagonal pieces
4 ounces (125 g) blood sausage, diced

Put the stock, liver sausage, savory, and sage in a deep saucepan, and cook gently until the sausage falls apart, about 20 minutes. Stir from time to time to break up the meat. Skim off any scum that forms as the sausage cooks. While the liver sausage is cooking, mix the coriander-flavored sausage and veal sausage in a skillet, and sauté over medium heat until the meat begins to brown. Lift out with a slotted spoon and reserve. Discard excess fat. Once the stock is heated and the liver sausage is blended into the soup, add the browned sausages and the diced blood sausage. Cook 5 minutes, or until the sausages are hot. Serve immediately.

Pork Stock for Metzelsupp

YIELD: 3 1/2 quarts (3 1/2 liters)

3 1/2 pounds (1 3/4 kg) meaty pork bones
1 small carrot, cut in half lengthwise
1 medium onion, cut in half and stuck with 6 cloves
2 pods hot pepper (preferably cayenne-type)
1 fresh bouquet garni (5 small sprigs marjoram, 1 sprig rosemary,
    3 sprigs parsley), or 1 1/2 tablespoons of the dried commercial mix
5 fresh bay leaves, bruised

Put all the ingredients except the bouquet garni and bay leaves in a deep stewing pan with 1 gallon (4 liters) of water, and bring to a boil over medium-high heat. Remove any scum that forms as the stock begins to boil. Reduce the heat and simmer gently for 2 hours, adding the bouquet garni and bay leaves about 30 minutes toward the end. Strain the stock, and pick the meat from the bones. Reserve the meat for soups or dumplings, or add a little to the *Metzelsupp.* Refrigerate the stock so that it cools and jells, then skim off the fat. Freeze or use as needed.

9. Pepper Hash for Scrapple

Pepper hash, or Philadelphia relish, was made in Philadelphia as early as the 1840s and quickly spread into the surrounding country-side once canning jars came into fashion. There were two kinds, one cooked, the other a raw marinade. Some recipes included minced cabbage; all of them were sweet-and-sour. Their popularity in hotels, cafeterias, schools, and boardinghouses may be gauged by Emma Smedley's large-batch recipe for fifty people, which appeared in her 1904 *Institution Recipes.* The recipe below, from the same period, is a cooked variation without cabbage that comes from Bethlehem, Pennsylvania.[68] Like Smedley's Philadelphia relish, this hash was intended to be served with scrapple. The match is classic.

YIELD: 4 to 4 1/2 pints (1 to 1 1/4 liters)

4 1/2 cups (675 g) finely chopped green bell pepper
4 1/2 cups (675 g) finely chopped red bell pepper
4 1/2 cups (500 g) finely chopped onion
2 small pods hot pepper, seeded and finely chopped
1 1/2 tablespoons celery seed
1 1/2 cups (375 ml) cider vinegar
1 1/2 cups (250 g) brown sugar
1 1/2 teaspoons sea salt or pickling salt

Combine the bell peppers, onion, hot pepper, and celery seed in a nonreactive preserving kettle. Heat the vinegar in a nonreactive pan, and dissolve the sugar and salt in it. Bring to a hard boil, then pour over the pepper mixture. Cook over medium heat for 15 minutes, or until the peppers begin to discolor. Pack into hot, sterilized canning jars. Place jars in a 15-minute water bath. Let the hash mature in the jars for 2 weeks before using.

10. Pocono Chicken Scrapple (Jewish Style)

Kasza is Polish for grits. The word does not refer to any particular grain, although in the United States, especially among American Jews, the term is used almost exclusively for buckwheat. Millet *kasza* was the grain of choice in medieval Poland; *kasza gryczana* (buckwheat grits) was a poverty food.[69] Most of the modern Polish dishes based on buckwheat originated in western Russia or Lithuania, but when Polish Jews came to America, they brought with them the buckwheat cookery that reminded them of their life in the villages and Jewish ghettos of old Poland.

Scrapple made with buckwheat groats, the toasted whole seeds, is not a far stretch from some of the traditional Jewish foods of Central Europe, but it also represents an interesting adaptation to something essentially American. The nutty flavor is delightful. Be sure when shopping for kasha that you purchase the whole groats, although the recipe will work if cracked buckwheat is employed. This recipe will use up the entire contents of one 16-ounce package of groats; keep that in mind when shopping. The Pocono brand of buckwheat groats, which used to be produced in Pennsylvania, is now owned by Birkett Mills of Penn Yan, New York. Many other brands are also available, especially in health food and natural food stores. Look for them in the section devoted to breakfast foods.

Many Jews, like the Pennsylvania Dutch, prefer to cook with chicken feet because they give the stock a rich flavor. You do not have to use chicken feet; they are entirely optional. For kosher Jews, who cannot use butter (the original recipe used margarine), chicken or goose fat is the best choice; olive oil will change the texture and flavor slightly but can be used as a substitute.

YIELD: 18 to 20 servings

2 pounds (1 kg) chicken thighs (or other parts) with skin
2 chicken feet (optional)
1 cup (150 g) chopped onion
2 eggs
2 1/2 cups (435 g) whole buckwheat groats (kasha)
4 tablespoons (60 g) chicken fat or butter
1/2 cup (75 g) yellow cornmeal
1 teaspoon freshly grated black pepper
1/2 tablespoon minced fresh rosemary (or 1 teaspoon dried)

Put the chicken thighs, feet, and onion in a large stewing pan with 2 1/2 quarts (2 1/2 liters) of water. Bring to a gentle boil over medium heat and cook for 1 hour, or until the meat falls from the bones. Skim off any fat that rises to the surface. Strain the stock and reserve. Separate the meat, discarding bones and other inedible parts. Chop the chicken and onion mixture and reserve. Beat 2 eggs until lemon colored, and combine with the kasha. Stir to coat the groats with the egg, and set aside to dry for 15 minutes. Then heat the chicken fat or butter, and brown the kasha for 5 minutes in a heavy stewing pan, or until the mixture looks wet and smells nutty. Add the reserved chicken stock and cover. Cook over medium heat for 20 minutes, or until the kasha becomes thick and the grains have burst. Add the ground chicken, cornmeal, black pepper, and rosemary. Stir vigorously until the mixture is stiff and ropy, at least 10 minutes, then pour into a large bread pan. Cool on a rack for 2 to 3 hours, then refrigerate. The next day, turn out the scrapple, slice, and fry in a lightly greased skillet until golden brown on both sides.

11. Poor-Do (Hawkins County, Tennessee)

There is no fixed way to make poor-do, because it is normally pre-pared with leftovers; the basic ingredients are whatever is on hand. Yet there are some consistent elements, and this recipe from the Clinch Mountain area, southwest of Kingsport, Tennessee, contains most of them. Pork fatback or bacon is essential. White cowpeas or greasy beans give it added flavor. Cornbread crumbs take the place of cornmeal, although cornmeal can be used. Unlike scrapple, where the cornmeal is added at the end, poor-do reverses the procedure by adding the stock last. It is basically a stew cooked until thick, but a poor man's stew for certain. A variant of this recipe, from a place near Chalk Level on the Holston River, calls for squirrel instead of pork. Just substitute 1 pound (500 g) of dressed squirrel for the pork—that would be the meatiest parts of about 3 squirrels. For best flavor, mar-inate the squirrel in beer 1 hour before cooking.

YIELD: 18 to 20 servings

1 pound (500 g) pork or squirrel
1/2 pound (250 g) pork fatback or fatty bacon (weight after
    rind is trimmed off)
2 cups (400 g) cooked cowpeas (preferably a white crowder
    variety)
1 cup (150 g) chopped onion
3 cups (300 g) grated cornbread crumbs (stale or day-old)
1/2 cup (75 g) old-fashioned hominy grits
1 teaspoon salt or to taste
2 teaspoons freshly ground black pepper

Bring 2 quarts (2 liters) of water to a boil in a large stewing pan. Add the pork or squirrel and the fatback. Boil 20 minutes over medium heat, skimming off any fat that rises to the surface. Remove the fatback, cut into small dice, and reserve. Continue cooking the pork or squirrel for an additional 40 minutes, or until the stock is reduced by half. Strain the stock, measure to be certain that it is 1 quart (1 liter), and reserve. If cooking squirrel, pick the meat from the bones. Grind the pork or squirrel so that it resembles sausage, then combine this with the cooked cowpeas. Mash the meat and cowpeas together to form a paste.

Clean the stewing pan, and add the diced fatback and onion. Cook over medium-high heat for 8 minutes, or until the onion is soft and turning golden, then add the meat and cowpea mixture. Cook for 5 minutes over medium-high heat, stirring occasionally to keep it from sticking, then add the cornbread crumbs, hominy grits, salt, and pepper. Stir-fry the mixture for 5 minutes, then add the reserved stock. Stir almost continuously for 25 to 30 minutes, or until the mixture becomes thick like mashed potatoes. The more it is stirred, the better the texture. Serve as a hot porridge, or pour into a lightly greased pan and set aside to cool. Once cool, refrigerate overnight. The next day, slice, dust with cornmeal, and fry like scrapple.

12. Potawatomi Beef Scrapple (Oklahoma)

This recipe surfaced near Shawnee, Oklahoma, and comes from a family that has been making it off and on since the 1920s. Family tradition holds that the recipe is much older than that, which is quite possible. Though this is a crossover recipe from a nineteenth-century cookbook, there are so many local adjustments that it would be fair to put it on a par with Chickasaw *pashofa* and other similar dishes. In fact, this recipe may be an echo of something once prepared with buffalo, which can be easily substituted for the ground beef. The use of coarsely ground corn gives the dish an interesting flavor and texture. As one of the family pointed out to me, their grandmother used to collect nodding onions *(Allium cernuum)* for her scrapple, wild onions with shallotlike bulbs tasting strongly of garlic. Nodding onions are the ramps of the Great Plains, and there is no mistake about the pungent flavor.

YIELD: 2 large loaves, 18 to 20 servings each

2 pounds (1 kg) ground beef
1 cup (150 g) chopped onion
1/2 cup (75 g) chopped shallots (or nodding onions
    for the adventuresome)
1 tablespoon salt
2 teaspoons freshly grated black pepper
1 cup (150 g) cooked beans (such as kidney beans)
2 cups (350 g) cooked sweet or shoepeg corn
3 cups (465 g) yellow cornmeal

Bring 2 1/2 quarts (2 1/2 liters) of water to a boil in a heavy 4-quart (4-liter) stewing pot. Add the meat, onion, and shallots. Boil gently over medium heat 40 minutes, skimming off any scum that rises to the surface. Strain out the meat and onion mixture, and return the stock to the pot. Chop or grind the meat and onions to an even consistency, and return to the stock. Add the salt and pepper. Grind the beans to a puree and add to the stock. Shred or chop the cooked corn to break up the kernels so that they resemble grated corn, then add this to the stock. Gradually sift in the cornmeal, alternating between sifting and stirring to avoid lumps. Then stir vigorously so that the mixture thickens and becomes ropy (about 15 to 20 minutes). Continue cooking and stirring for 20 minutes, so that most of the moisture is cooked out. Pour into a lightly greased pan, and set on a rack to cool. Refrigerate overnight. The next day, remove from the pan, slice, and brown in a skillet lightly brushed with oil.

13. Scrabblin' Mush, or Rice Scrapple (South Carolina)

Carolina rice scrapple reminds me of the natural remains of hoppin' john reincarnated into something similar in texture to goetta. The mild climate of the coastal country allows cooks to have fresh bay leaves and rosemary by the kitchen doorstep all year round, and it is no surprise that both of these fragrant herbs show up in even the simplest of recipes. Since much of the flavor of rice scrapple is in the boiling stock, you might consider using a traditional Charleston soup bunch. This is a bouquet of herbs and vegetables tied up with string, consisting of parsley, a slice or two of squash, some spring onions or small leeks, a few bay leaves on the stem, and a small parsnip. It is removed when the stock is strained.

YIELD: 28 to 30 servings

2 pounds (1 kg) fresh pork, preferably ground sausage
   without seasonings
5 or 6 fresh bay leaves, bruised
6-inch (15 cm) sprig of fresh rosemary (optional)
1 cup (150 g) chopped onion
1 cup (200 g) cooked black-eyed peas
3 cups (450 g) cooked day-old rice
1 cup (150 g) white cornmeal
2 teaspoons freshly grated black pepper

Bring 2 quarts (2 liters) of water to boil in a large stewing pan. Add the pork, bay leaves, rosemary, and onion. Cook over medium-high heat for 45 minutes, or until the meat is tender. Strain the stock, and return to the stewing pan. Discard the rosemary and bay leaves. Grind the meat, onion, and black-eyed peas to an even texture, then add this to the stock, along with the rice, cornmeal, and pepper. Cook the mixture over medium heat for 30 to 40 minutes, or until thick like mashed potatoes, stirring almost continuously so that it does not stick to the bottom. Pour into lightly greased pans, and cool on racks. Once the mush has cooled, cover and refrigerate. The next day, remove from the pans, slice, dust with cornmeal, and fry like scrapple.

14. South Street Scrapple

South Street, Philadelphia, has a culture all its own, a bit like London's Soho with a dash of punk and New Orleans sleaze. The neighborhood also marks the northernmost border of what locals refer to as South Philly, which is where the city's Italian community is concentrated. That community has been a breeding ground for fascinating culinary hybrids, such as scrapple made with *luganega,* a spicy Italian sausage sold in a long coil. South Street scrapple looks vaguely like polenta and tastes like pizza, but the premise is not too different from Frank Corriher's hot liver mush, which is a hit down in North Carolina. This culinary trend toward spiciness is probably a reflection of the growing Latinization of American cooking on all levels. And while South Street Scrapple is not the scrapple that scrapple

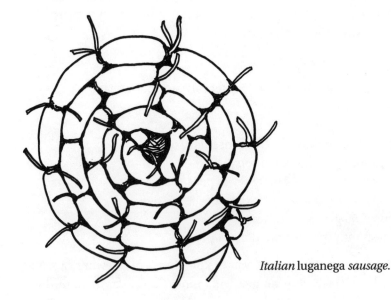

Italian luganega *sausage.*

lovers love most, it has appeared on hip restaurant menus as far away as Chicago and Denver. Trendy bistros aside, the preferred way of eating it is with lots of grilled onions and grilled green peppers. Add some arugula if you like.

YIELD: approximately 18 to 20 servings

1 pound (500 g) fresh (uncooked) spicy Italian sausage
1 cup (150 g) chopped onion
1 cup (150 g) dry sausage (such as pepperoni), cut into tiny dice
1 teaspoon salt
1 teaspoon coarsely ground pepper
2 teaspoons ground marjoram or oregano
1 tablespoon ground coriander (optional)
3 cups (465 g) yellow cornmeal

Bring $2^1/2$ quarts ($2^1/2$ liters) of water to boil in a heavy 3- or 4-quart (3- or 4-liter) stewing pan. Cut the sausage into irregular pieces, and add to the water along with the onion. Boil gently over medium heat for 40 minutes, skimming off any fat that rises to the surface. Lift out the sausage with a slotted spoon and remove the skins. If the sausage does not break apart easily, chop it in a food processor until it achieves a fine, even texture. Pour this back into the cooking stock. Add the diced dry sausage and seasonings. Gradually sift in the cornmeal, alternating between sifting and stirring to avoid lumps. Then stir vigorously so that the mixture thickens and becomes ropy (about 15 to 20 minutes). Once the scrapple thickens, pour it into a lightly greased bread pan, filling to the top. Set on a rack to cool, then refrigerate overnight. The next day, slice and brown in a skillet lightly brushed with oil.

Note: Italian sausage normally contains a large amount of annatto (achiote) and paprika, both of which give it a red color. This coloring will change the scrapple to a deep orange-yellow, one of the distinctive features of this recipe. While the herbs and spices are all a matter of personal taste, it is important to read the sausage label to determine what spices are already in the sausage so that you do not over-spice the scrapple. Authentic Italian *luganega* contains parmesan cheese, but most American versions dispense with it; the cheese is not an essential component of this recipe.

15. Tarheel Liver Mush

The working recipe from which this has been adapted originated in Hickory, North Carolina, an old family recipe that used much more of the pig than is required here. The taste and texture are very close to the original, however. The predominant flavor is liver, somewhere between liverwurst and scrapple. All liver mush recipes are quite flexible, and some people add a much higher proportion of other meat products, though commercial liver mush must contain at least 30 percent pork liver. Most of the ingredients for liver mush are not generally available in supermarkets and must be purchased from a butcher. Pork hearts are ideal because they cook soft after an hour of stewing and, when ground to a paste with the other meats, give the liver mush a more even texture. If you prefer to make liver pudding instead, the recipe is below.

YIELD: 2 loaves, 18 to 20 servings each

3 pounds (1½ kg) fresh pork liver
1 pound (500 g) pork heart
¾ pound (375 g) unseasoned freshly ground pork sausage
    or ground pork side meat
1 tablespoon salt
1 tablespoon ground sage
1 teaspoon black pepper
½ teaspoon cayenne pepper, or to taste
3 cups (465 g) cornmeal

Cut the liver and heart into large, irregular pieces. Put in a 3- or 4-quart (3- or 4-liter) stewing pan with the sausage or ground side meat. Add 2½ quarts (2½ liters) of water, and bring to a boil over medium-high heat. Skim off any scum that may rise to the surface. Cook the meat 1 hour, or until the heart is tender, then strain all the meat from the broth. Return the broth to the stewing pan. Pick out the pieces of liver from the strained meat, and coarsely grind half of it. Grind the rest of the liver with the remaining meat until it attains the consistency of a fine paste. Add the ground meats to the strained broth along with the seasonings. Bring to a gentle boil over medium heat. Gradually sift in the cornmeal, stirring as you sift so that it does not form lumps. Cook and stir constantly for about 20 to 30 minutes, or until the liver mush attains a thick, ropy consistency. Pour into lightly greased pans to cool, then refrigerate overnight. Turn out into a glass platter or baking dish. Cover and refrigerate until needed. Slice and serve cold or fry in a skillet like scrapple. For a crispier crust, dust the slices with flour before frying.

Liver Pudding

To convert the recipe to liver pudding, omit the cornmeal and add an additional pound (500 g) of pork heart plus 1 pig's foot. Boil the foot with the rest of the meats for 1 hour, and use the meat from the foot in the pudding. If a pig's foot is not available, dissolve 8 packets of clear, unflavored gelatin in the strained stock. Grind the meat as directed for liver mush, add it to the stock with the seasonings, cook 25 minutes, and pour the pudding into pans. Refrigerate until stiff. This will yield 2 pans of coarse aspic, which can be sliced and eaten cold, or heated to make a thick gravy for grits, toast, mashed potatoes, hash browns, or boiled rice, or an Amish-style sauce for scrapple.

16. Tomato Butter for Scrapple, or Scrapple Butter

This scrapple classic is based on a recipe published in 1911 by Mrs. William Long of the Grace Reformed Ladies' Aid Society in Millgrove, Pennsylvania. It is the kind of recipe I work on while I am doing other things in the kitchen. The effort is worth it, because scrapple butter is much better than catsup and easily doubles as a first-rate barbecue or basting sauce. It can also be mixed with mustard.

YIELD: 1 quart (1 liter)

4 pounds (2 kg) ripe paste tomatoes
1 pound (500 g) dark brown sugar
1 cup (250 ml) red wine vinegar
2 teaspoons pickling salt
grated rind plus juice of 1/2 lemon
1/2 teaspoon ground cloves
1/2 teaspoon ground cinnamon

Wash and chop the tomatoes. Cook them in a deep preserving pan with a little water until completely soft, about 25 minutes, then press through a colander or strainer to remove the skins and seeds. Return the strained tomato to the pan, and add the sugar, vinegar, and salt. Boil over medium heat for 1 1/2 hours, then add the lemon and spices. Stir at regular intervals as the butter thickens to keep it from scorching on the bottom. Frequent stirring also increases evaporation and hastens thickening. The tomato butter should be ready to put up in hot, sterilized jars in about 2 hours.

17. Vegetarian Mushroom–Wild Rice Scrapple

Vegetarians have been eating meatless scrapples for more than a hundred years, so there is nothing unusual about making a vegan scrapple that is the philosophical opposite of liver mush. I started making this recipe several years ago after being challenged to come up with something resembling Philadelphia-style scrapple without the pig. It has become quite popular, especially with scrapple lovers who want to eat scrapple during Lent.

YIELD: 28 to 30 servings

2 pounds (1 kg) mushrooms, cleaned and chopped
    into irregular pieces (portobello are ideal)
2 cups (400 g) cooked black beans
3 cups (525 g) cooked wild rice
1 tablespoon salt
1 tablespoon ground sage
1 tablespoon ground summer savory
2 teaspoons freshly ground black pepper
1/4 teaspoon cloves
1 cup (150 g) yellow cornmeal
1 cup (125 g) buckwheat flour

Bring 2 quarts (2 liters) of water to a rolling boil in a 4-quart (4-liter) stewing pan. Reduce the heat to medium, and add the mushrooms. Stew 40 minutes, or until the mushrooms are tender and fleshy in texture. Strain out the mushrooms, reserve 1 cup (250 ml) of stock, and return the remaining stock to the pan. Grind or chop the mushrooms to a ground beef consistency, then add them to the stock. Puree the cooked beans with the reserved stock, and add this to the mushrooms. Grind the cooked wild rice to a coarse grits texture, and add to the stock. Add the seasonings. Bring the stock to a gentle boil over medium heat. Once the stock begins to boil, sift together the cornmeal and buckwheat flour, then gradually sift this into the scrapple mixture. Stir almost continuously for 20 to 25 minutes, or until the scrapple attains a thick, mashed potato consistency. Pour into lightly greased pans to cool. Once cool, refrigerate overnight, then turn out of the pan. Slice and fry like scrapple.

Note: Because of the presence of mushrooms, this scrapple will not keep for any length of time. Store unused portions in the refrigerator, but do not keep for more than 4 days. Otherwise, freeze for later use according to freezing instructions given on page 82.

18. Venison Scrapple (Colorado)

In *The Food Journal of Lewis and Clark,* Mary Gunderson noted how scrapple moved west across the plains during the nineteenth and early twentieth centuries. Frontiersmen made scrapple from whatever game they could find, since it was, to quote Gunderson, the "pillar of ordinary foods."[70] A more recent chapter in this scrapple diaspora was related to me by Margaret Lauterbach of Boise, Idaho: "My grandmother was raised in Salisbury, Westmoreland County, Pennsylvania, and as a young woman she boarded a train and left for eastern Colorado, where she wed her former schoolteacher. Her name was Estella Ferrell, and she married Robert McCutcheon in 1906, and then remained in Colorado all her life. She had four brothers back in Pennsylvania but never returned because she was expected to do everything for them. My dad hunted venison during the World War II meat shortages, so she had that venison. He ate beef while the rest of the family ate venison, since she made a lot of it into venison scrapple, which she had learned to make in Pennsylvania."[71]

YIELD: 2 loaves, 18 to 20 servings each

2 pounds (1 kg) venison, cut into cubes for stewing
juice of 2 limes
1/2 pound (250 g) slab bacon, coarsely chopped
   (weight after rind is removed)
1 cup (150 g) chopped onions
4 cloves garlic, chopped
3 large sprigs fresh rosemary (2 tablespoons dry)
1 tablespoon salt
2 teaspoons freshly ground pepper
2 teaspoons ground allspice
1 tablespoon thyme leaves
3 cups (465 g) yellow cornmeal

Two hours before making the scrapple, put the venison in a nonreactive bowl and sprinkle liberally with lime juice. Marinate the meat in the juice; after 2 hours, discard the excess liquid. To make the scrapple, bring 2 quarts (2 liters) of water to a rolling boil in a 4-quart

(4-liter) stewing pan. Add the venison, bacon, onions, garlic, and rosemary. Stew over medium heat for 1 hour, then strain the stock. Return the stock to the stewing pan. Discard the sprigs of rosemary. Grind the meat, onions, and garlic to a ground beef consistency, then return this to the stock. Add the salt, pepper, allspice, and thyme. Bring the mixture to a gentle boil over medium heat, then gradually sift in the cornmeal, stirring as it is added to avoid lumps. Cook the scrapple for 25 to 30 minutes, stirring constantly, until it becomes thick like mashed potatoes. Pour into a greased pan to cool. When cool, cover and refrigerate. The next day, remove from the pan, slice, and fry in a lightly greased skillet.

19. Westphalian *Panhas* (Stovetop Version)

This recipe comes from Käthe Schnichels of Blankenheim-Ripsdorf in the North Eifel region of Nordrhein-Westfalen. It was supplied by Dr. Dieter Pesch of the Rheinisches Freilichtmuseum/Landesmuseum für Volkskunde (Kommern, Germany). The translation is mine. This early-twentieth-century recipe, like those found in German cookbooks, adapts the process to ingredients readily available from butcher shops.

YIELD: 18 to 20 servings

1 quart (1 liter) sausage stock (white stock)
2 ounces (65 g) pork side meat or fatback
2 medium onions
8 ounces (250 g) blood sausage *(Blutwurst)*
8 ounces (250 g) liver sausage *(Leberwurst)*
salt and pepper to taste
3 to 4 cups (375 to 500 g) sifted buckwheat flour
1/2 teaspoon ground cloves
ground marjoram or oregano to taste (2 to 3 teaspoons
    recommended)

Put the stock in a heavy stewing pan, and bring to a boil. Chop or grind the side meat and onions to a fine paste. Remove the skins from the *Blutwurst* and *Leberwurst,* and chop into coarse pieces. Add all the chopped ingredients to the stock, and boil gently over medium heat until the side meat is soft and the sausages have dissolved, about 25 to 30 minutes. Add the salt and pepper, and gradually stir in the buckwheat flour. Once the mixture begins to thicken, add the cloves and marjoram or oregano. Continue stirring until the mixture is so thick that the stirring spoon stands on its own in the pan. Pour into a well-greased bread pan, and stand in a refrigerator overnight or until the *Panhas* sets. Slice as needed, and fry in a lightly greased skillet.

20. Zucchini Relish for Scrapple

My grandmother, Grace Hickman Weaver, developed this recipe in her head over the course of several years, until she got it where she wanted it to pair off with her weekly dose of scrapple. The recipe was never written down. She stopped making the relish when she turned ninety-six, and that is when I offered to take over the job—in part to get the recipe before it was lost. Scrapple relish should not be too sweet, one of the faults of many commercial relishes today. The bonus with this recipe is that it makes good use of those oversize zucchinis that mysteriously appear in the garden, and for which many gardeners are hard-pressed to find a use. Well, here is the happy solution.

YIELD: 6 pint jars (3 liters)

8 cups (1 kg) finely diced mature zucchini
4 cups (600 g) finely chopped onion
1 1/2 cups (200 g) finely diced green bell pepper
1 1/2 cups (200 g) finely diced sweet red pepper
1/2 cup (125 g) salt
3 cups (750 g) sugar
2 1/2 cups (375 ml) vinegar
1 cup (250 ml) spring water
2 tablespoons turmeric
2 tablespoons celery seed

Mix the zucchini, onion, peppers, and salt in a large mixing bowl. Cover with cold spring water and ice cubes. Let stand 1 hour, then drain and rinse lightly in a colander. Put the zucchini mixture in a deep preserving pan. Heat the sugar, vinegar, 1 cup spring water, turmeric, and celery seed in a nonreactive preserving pan. Boil hard for 3 minutes, then pour over the zucchini mixture. Cook slowly over medium heat for 15 minutes, or until the zucchini is tender but not soft. Transfer to hot, sanitized canning jars, and seal.

Scrapple Terminology

Balkenbrij. A Holland Dutch word for scrapple. The term derives from the Old Dutch *balge,* a word cognate with English *bacon.* In the United States, this term is recorded only in the nineteenth-century Dutch settlements around Holland, Michigan. It was used there as a local term for American-style scrapple. In the Netherlands, *balkenbrij* is legally recognized by the European Union as a regional food product. It can be made and sold only by certified butchers.

Breimehl. A *Pennsylfaanisch* word for the flour and meal mix used to thicken the butcher's broth. The term consists of two words, *Brei* (gruel) and *Mehl* (flour or meal). In Westphalia, the typical *Breimehl* consists of a mixture of fine oatmeal and buckwheat flour. In Pennsylvania, it consists of cornmeal and buckwheat flour.

Buckwheat. Buckwheat *(Fagopyrum esculentum)* is not a cereal grain, but a plant more closely related to rhubarb than to any of the grains with which it is mixed to make scrapple. The plant originated in Yunnan Province, China, and slowly moved westward across Asia until it reached Europe in the Middle Ages. It did not become firmly established in the German diet until the 1600s. In parts of Westphalia, buckwheat is called *Heidekorn* (heath wheat), in reference to its cultivation on marginal soils.

Butcher broth. The white stock left over after boiling sausages. See *Metzelsupp.*

Cornmeal. Any type of mill-ground corn. Many traditional textures are not readily available today.

Crust. This is the crisp texture on the exterior of a fried slice of scrapple. The delicate quality of the crust, its color, and its flavor are important factors in determining the quality of a scrapple product.

German scrapple. A common term used commercially and on the Internet for *Götta, Grötta,* or goetta, scrapple made with oatmeal. This type of scrapple originated in the Osnabrück region of Germany and is a close relative of Westphalian *Panhas.*

Goetta. A commercially registered name with the USDA for oatmeal scrapple. This type of scrapple is popular in northern Kentucky and parts of Ohio. In Ohio, its production centers around Cincinnati and Toledo. See German Scrapple.

Haslet. This word sometimes appears in old manuscript cookery books as *harslet.* This was a cut of organ meat generally consisting of the heart, liver, and lights (lungs), connected together as one loose piece by the "windpipe." Butchers treated lamb, pork, and veal haslets with varying degrees of culinary merit. Veal haslets were considered the very finest. Lamb or sheep haslet was most often called the *pluck,* although this term also applied to haslets in general, especially in American speech prior to the 1830s. The fact that the haslet was considered a delicacy is well documented in medieval cookery books, which normally mention it as spit-roasted. In the *Forme of Cury,* dating from the 1390s, there is a recipe for *hasteletes of fruyt.* This is a mixture of dried fruits molded to resemble a haslet and eaten during Lent.

Head cheese. An aspic made from a cleaned pig's head and tongue. The brains, eyes, and snout are removed. Most of the meat used comes from the exterior part of the skull. Vinegar is commonly added, as well as herbs and spices. There are several British Isle equivalents, such as Welsh brawn *(cosyn pen).* It is common practice to place a weight on the meat to press it while it cools and stiffens. It is this pressing action that gives it the name "cheese." In France, head cheese is called *fromage de tête de porc*, and it is customary to line the aspic pan with bacon before filling it with the mixture. This bacon coating keeps the aspic from drying out once it is removed from the pan.

Hot meat, hot chop, or hot bone processing. This is a butchering term for the most traditional way to prepare pork products, especially sausages and scrapple, and means that processing begins while the animal is still warm after butchering. This can be done only with small-batch slaughtering of a few animals at a time. Large slaughterhouses and meat processors cannot accommodate this method; there the meat is refrigerated after butchering and is processed cold. Hot meat processing yields a far superior meat product in terms of flavor and texture. A good analogy would be the difference in flavor between a fish caught and cooked immediately and one that has been held on ice for several days. As with all food products, it is freshness that determines real quality.

Liver mush. A type of scrapple commonly associated with the North Carolina Piedmont and sections of northern South Carolina, although it is found as far south as Georgia and northern Alabama. Recipes vary, but liver mush, also called pork mush, may be roughly defined as a pot pudding thickened with a cereal, usually cornmeal. It does not contain buckwheat flour. It is eaten either cold or fried like Pennsylvania scrapple. There are more than fifteen commercial liver mush producers in the Piedmont South.

Liver pudding. These foot-long sausages, called *Lewwerwarscht* in *Pennsylfaanisch*, were popular among urban working classes and thus were a source of easy cash for farmers. The urban poor mashed and cooked the puddings with crackers to make a thick winter porridge that could be served alone or poured like gravy over boiled potatoes. Liver puddings sold in casings are generally referred to as "skin puddings" in Pennsylvania and Maryland.

In the South, liver pudding is a pot pudding consisting of all pork products. It contains no cereal thickening and generally no other seasoning than salt and pepper. The binding agent is gelatin from skin and bones, so it melts and falls apart when heated. Liver pudding is also used in some parts of the South to refer to liver mush.

Metzelsupp. This word has three basic meanings sometimes used interchangeably. The primary meaning is the stock that remains after making sausages during butchering. This is also known as the "white broth" and serves as the basis for making scrapple. The second meaning is the butchering-day soup that is made from the white broth and served to the people who helped with butchering activities. The manner in which this soup is made and the way it is served vary from region to region. The third meaning is the gift of sausages, scrapple, and soup that is sent home with the people who helped with butchering or distributed to the needy in the neighborhood. In Pennsylvania, *Metzelsupp* evolved into the name for food gifts given to people at Christmas.

Mundle. A southeastern Pennsylvania term deriving from the Welsh *myndl.* It signifies a pot stick for stirring mush, gruel, or scrapple. The mundle was made of oak, gum, or some type of hardwood. An alternate term, *nooden,* is documented in the 1702 manuscript cookery book of William Penn's wife. A Westphalian word, *Pannhasrührer* (scrapple stirrer), has been recorded in some areas of northwest Germany. This applied to a special tool with metal flanges on one end, but the word and tool were evidently rare, since any sort of large, multipurpose pot stick could be employed for the task.

Mush. A common term in the Middle States for gruel, especially cornmeal gruel eaten hot like porridge or allowed to cool and then sliced and fried like scrapple. The full, proper Pennsylvania High German term for cornmeal mush was *Welschkornmehlbrei.* A detailed recipe for making it appeared in the *Neuer Gemeinnütziger Pennsylvanischer Calender* (The New Pennsylvania Almanac for General Use) published in Lancaster, Pennsylvania, in 1892. One of the first printed recipes for making mush appeared in Mary Randolph's *Virginia House-Wife* in 1824.

National Scrapple Day. Urban legend. This is an unofficial date that has gained currency due to its repeated inclusion on Internet calendars. The date is generally given as November 9, although this day has no significant connection with any time in the history of scrapple. During the Middle Ages, early November was commonly associated with fall butchering prior to a period of forty days of fasting that ended on Christmas Eve.

Oats. The *Pennsylfaanisch* term is *Haber* or *Hawwer.* Oats *(Avena sativa)* was a grain associated with poverty foods in Germany, and for this reason, it was generally avoided by the German settlers in Pennsylvania. According to the Sauer herbal, oat flour soups were considered beneficial for the sick, but beyond that, oats did not figure in cookery, and especially not in Pennsylvania scrapple. In northern Germany, however, where oat consumption continued into the nineteenth century, oat-based porridges and scrapples became associated with regional fare.

Immigrants from that part of Germany brought an oat-based scrapple called *götta* or *grötta* (meaning groats or grits) to a number of settlements in Ohio and the Midwest, where the dish is still prepared. See Goetta.

Pan. For molding *Panhas*, there were two traditional types of pans. The oldest medieval forms were squat and round, with flat bottoms and straight sides, resembling a saucepan without a handle. This form was continued in America in both redware and salt-glaze versions. An alternate shape, which was imitated by commercial scrapple makers, was the so-called loaf pan. Dated examples from Westphalia can be traced to the mid-1600s, although the form is considerably older. It is the same type of earthenware pan used to make French terrines.

Panhas or **Pannas.** A Westphalian dialect term for scrapple. It is a loan word in *Pennsylfaanisch* that derives mostly from south German dialects such as Swabian and Palatine German. *Panhas* derives from *panna*, the name for the cooking utensil in which it was made. Many country butchers in the United States use *Panhas* interchangeably with scrapple, and there is a wide variety of spellings. Other butchers differentiate between *Panhas* and scrapple, explaining that *Panhas* contains more meat and less flour than scrapple, but in fact they are variations of the same thing. *Panhas* normally contains pork blood as well as ground meat.

Pannage. This term is of Celto-Roman origin. As defined by *The Farmer's Encyclopaedia* (1844), it is an old manorial term applied to the food that swine consume in woods, such as acorns or beechnuts. It also signifies the money taken by the king's agistors for the privi-

Panhas, *otherwise known as scrapple, is sold in many parts of rural America. This sign stands along Route 23 in Delaware, Ohio.* PHOTO AND BROCHURE MOM WILSON COUNTRY SAUSAGE MART

lege of feeding hogs in his forest. The Penns attempted to collect a pannage tax on their manor lands in Pennsylvania prior to the Revolution but found the tithe unenforceable. In colonial America, pannage was highly valued as fodder for pigs allowed to roam freely in the woods. Acorn-fed pigs produce the best-tasting hams and scrapple. Pannage is the secret to the flavor of Spain's famous *jamón ibérico* (Iberian ham).

Panne. French for unrendered hog's lard. The equivalent term in German is *Filz* or *rohes Schweinefett.* Once the lard is rendered, it becomes *saindoux* in French. It is interesting that *panne* still retains a connection to pigs and may offer further etymological keys to understanding ancient forms of *pannas.*

Pfannengrütze or ***Pannegetta.*** One of several Lower Rhineland names for the Ohio and Kentucky scrapple called goetta.

Poor-do. An Appalachian term for scrapple most likely deriving from the Middle English verb *poure-to:* to mix together.

Pot pudding. Any sort of pork-and-liver pudding poured into a crock. Its modern equivalent is pan pudding, since it is now sold in tin or aluminum pans. In Pennsylvania, pot pudding is baked so that the fat rises to the top. The fat is then drained off, and the pudding is baked until a brown crust forms. Baked pot pudding is much lower in fat content than a liver pudding made by open-pot boiling. Pot pudding is also stuffed into large casings and tied into a ring. This is boiled in its own broth and sold as liver pudding. The broth is then used as a basis for scrapple.

Pudding meat. A term often applied to liver pudding, especially to meaty pot puddings. Many butchers reserve pudding meat to add to scrapple to give it a meatier taste.

Scrabblin' mush. A name for rice scrapple used in the South Carolina Low Country and in parts of coastal Georgia. It is also written scrapplin' mush and may derive from medieval English *scrapple,* a term for leftovers.

Scrapple. From *Kreppel,* a Low German dialect term for a small (or thin) slice of pot pudding, as in *Panhaskreppel.* Mush or *Panhas* fried on a hoe or shovel used like a hanging griddle was known as a *schrapelkoekje* (hoecake) in New Netherlands Dutch. The difference in meaning between *Kreppel* and *schrapel* became blurred in the spoken English of the Delaware Valley, because both terms sounded like the medieval English word *scrapple,* a term for leftovers.

Silver scrapple knives made in Philadelphia, c. 1875. From a set of twelve. In shape, the knife blade follows the style of seventeenth-century knives. ROUGHWOOD COLLECTION

Scrapple knife. A silver knife resembling a large fruit knife designed for slicing scrapple. Used as part of the breakfast service at formal breakfasts in Philadelphia and Baltimore.

Scrapple slice. A silver serving implement resembling a fish slice but more rectangular to fit the shape of sliced scrapple. It was used by the butler to transfer hot, cooked scrapple from the serving platter to individual plates.

Skins. Also called great skins, referring to large pork intestines. These were commonly used by the Pennsylvania Dutch for liver pudding (*Lewwerwarscht*).

Warschthorn (sausage horn). A *Pennsylfaanisch* term for a hollowed-out cow horn with the pointed end cut off so that it could be used as a funnel for stuffing sausages. The use of cow horns for this purpose is documented well into the early Middle Ages.

White broth. This is the stock left over after butchering, especially after boiling meat and sausages. It forms the basis for all scrapples.

Selected Listing of Scrapple, Liver Mush, and Goetta Producers

There are many producers of scrapple all over the United States, although the greatest number of them are concentrated in the Mid-Atlantic and Midwest regions. Surprisingly, Delaware is very much a center of scrapple making. Quite a few producers are small, family-owned firms that sell only to local clients; for a large number of country butchers, scrapple is a minor sideline, and they do not always list it among their products. For this reason, Internet listings can be misleading. All of the firms listed below sell scrapple unless otherwise stated. The purpose of this list is to help locate producers for readers who want to try scrapple without going through the trouble of making it themselves. This list is not exhaustive, and it does not imply an endorsement of the products, which vary greatly in taste and texture from region to region and from one firm to the next. However, all of the firms listed below have one thing in common: They care about their customers and are very willing to answer questions.

A. B. Wenger Meats
3433 Meadow View Rd.
Manheim, PA 17545-8317
(717) 653-4285
*Established 1958. Makes scrapple as custom work
as well as liver pudding.*

Alderfer Meats
382 Main St.
Harleysville, PA 19438
(215) 256-8818, toll-free (877) 253-6328
*Established 1922. Catalog, online ordering at
www.alderfermeats.com.*

The Amish Country Store
206 13th St. SW
Largo, FL 33770
(727) 587-9657
*Established 1997. Sells three brands of Pennsylvania-made
scrapple, liver pudding in rings, and pot pudding. Online
ordering at www.theamishcountrystore.com.*

Berks Packing Company
307–323 Bingman St.
P.O. Box 5919
Reading, PA 19610-5919
(610) 376-7291, (800) 882-3757
Established 1933. Online ordering at www.berksfoods.com.

Bixler's Meats
1585 E. Mountain Rd.
R.D. 1
Higgins, PA 17938
(570) 682-3449
Established 1960. Old-fashioned Philadelphia-style scrapple.

Bringhurst Meats, Inc.
38 W. Taunton Rd.
Berlin, NJ 08009
(856) 767-0110
*Established 1934. Catalog, online ordering at
www.bringhurstmeats.com.*

Carolina Pride
One Packer Ave.
Greenwood, SC 29646
(864) 229-5611
*Established 1920. Packages and distributes Carolina Pride
brand of liver mush. Website: www.carolinaprideonline.com.*

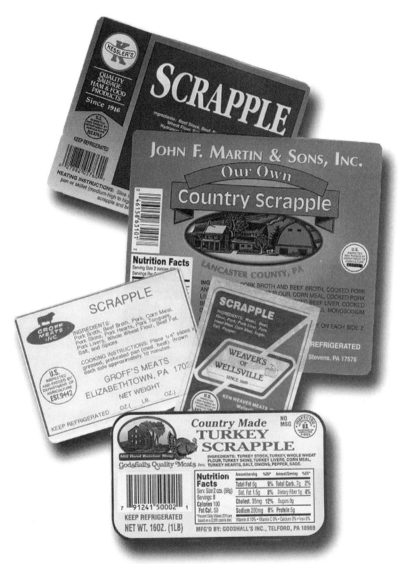

Scrapple labels are applied directly to the loaves of scrapple for retail selling. Labeling did not become common until the 1930s.

Clear Run Farms

Box 109, 45 Wilmington Highway
Harrells, NC 28444
(800) 863-7619
Established 1994. Liver pudding only. The Moore family, which operates the business, apprenticed under master liver pudding maker Garfield Cromartie.

Dietrich's Meats and Country Store
Old Rt. 22
Krumsville, PA 19534
(610) 756-6344; fax (610) 756-3480
Established 1975. Mail order. Pot pudding, liver pudding, and scrapple. Also at Renninger's Farm Market, Kutztown, Pennsylvania, on Fridays and Saturdays. Online information at www.dietrichs@renningers.com.

Dietz and Watson, Inc.
5701 Tacony St.
Philadelphia, PA 19135
(800) 333-1974
Established 1939. The only commercial maker of scrapple in Philadelphia. Catalog, online ordering at www.dietzandwatson.com.

Frank Corriher
Box 133
Landis, NC 28088
(704) 857-5519
Established 1936. Liver mush and hot, spicy liver mush, a much-sought-after local specialty. The firm also makes "souse meat."

Glier's Meats
533 Goetta Place
Covington, KY 41011
(859) 291-1800
Established 1946. Sells four types of goetta: original, beef, hot, and low-fat. Also sponsors each June a Goettafest in Goebel Park, Main Strasse Village, Covington, Kentucky. For details on the festival, call (859) 491-0458. Website: www.goetta.com.

Godshall's Quality Meats
675 Mill Rd.
Telford, PA 18969
(215) 256-8867 or (888) GODSHAL
Established 1945. Specializes in turkey products, including turkey scrapple and turkey liverwurst.

Groff's Meats, Inc.
33 N. Market St.
Elizabethtown, PA 17022
(717) 367-1246
Established 1875. Mail order and retail. Pot pudding and scrapple. Also well known for its mincemeat, which is served at the Apple-Scrapple Festival in Delaware.

Habbersett Sausage and Scrapple Company
701 Ashland Ave.
Folcroft, PA 19032
(610) 532-9973
Established 1863. Purchased in 1988 as a division of Jones Dairy Farm of Fort Atkinson, Wisconsin. Produces both pork and beef scrapple. Online ordering at www.habbersettscrapple.com.

Harrisonburg Wholesale Meat Company, Inc.
P.O. Box 82
256 Charles St.
Harrisonburg, VA 22803
(540) 434-4415
Established 1930. Sells scrapple under the commercial name Sterling Farms brand "pon-hoss" and pudding. Wholesale and retail.

Hatfield's Quality Meats, Inc.
2700 Funks Rd., Box 902
Hatfield, PA 19440-0902
(800) 743-1191
Established 1895. Online ordering at www.hatfieldqualitymeats.com.

Hoffman's Quality Meats
13225 Cearfoss Pike
Hagerstown, MD 21740
(800) 356-3193
Established 1923. Sells scrapple under the name "country pon haus" and pot pudding as "country pudding." Catalog and online ordering at www.hoffmanmeats.com.

Holland Brothers Meats
1279 Old Route 220 South
Duncansville, PA 16635-5318
(814) 695-5450
Established 1962. Makes scrapple and Panhas.

Horst Meats
17807 Reiff Church Rd.
Hagerstown, MD 21740
(301) 733-1089
Established 1975. Makes Panhas *and pudding in skins.*

Illg's Meats
365 Folly Rd.
Chalfont, PA 18914
(215) 343-0670
Established 1958. Online ordering at www.illgsmeats.com.

Jenkins Foods
2119 New House Rd.
Lattimore, NC 28150
(704) 434-2347
*Established 1933. Packages and distributes liver mush,
liver pudding, and scrapple.*

J. L. Miller Sons
490 Indian Rock Dam Rd.
York, PA 17403-9581
(717) 741-2431
Established 1940. Makes Panhas.

John F. Martin and Sons, Inc.
P.O. Box 137
Stevens, PA 17578
(717) 336-2804
*Established 1961. Makes scrapple for wholesale and
retail markets.*

Kessler's, Inc.
Box 126
Lemoyne, PA 17043
(717) 763-7162
Established 1916. Began selling scrapple in 1940. The firm also makes "pan pudding" (pot pudding). The stock for Kessler's scrapple is made from beef; thyme and sage are not used in the area.

Kirby and Holloway Provision Co.
966 Jackson Ditch Rd.
Harrington, DE 19952
(302) 398-3705
Established 1947. Produces a scrapple with more meat than traditional Pennsylvania scrapple, and uses white cornmeal like old-style Chesapeake scrapples.

Krall's Meat Market
326 E. Main St.
Schaefferstown, PA 17088
(717) 949-3411
Established 1932. Makes scrapple without a label. Makes liver pudding in casings marketed as "skin pudding."

Kunzler & Company, Inc.
652 Manor St.
Lancaster, PA 17604
(888) 586-9537
Established 1901. Scrapple recipes and online ordering at www.kunzler.com.

Leidy's, Inc.
266 Cherry Lane
P.O. Box 64257
Souderton, PA 18964
(215) 723-4606
Established 1893. Catalog and online ordering at www.Leidys.com.

Leninger's Quality Meats
Fairground Farmer's Market
2934 N. 5th St. Highway
Reading, PA 19606
(610) 921-2876
Established 1850. Only open Thursdays, Fridays, and Saturdays.

Mack's Livermush & Meats
6126 McKee Rd.
Shelby, NC 28150
(704) 434-6188
Established 1933. Mack's is responsible for establishing the first annual Livermush Expo in 1987. Retail and wholesale.

Milton Sausage & Scrapple Company LLC
113 Union St.
P.O. Box 308
Milton, DE 19968
(302) 684-8574
Established 1930. Milton uses whole wheat flour and cornmeal in its scrapple.

Mom Wilson's Country Sausage Mart
7720 U.S. 23 North
North Delaware, OH 43015
(740) 726-2636
Established 1959. The scrapple recipe has changed over the years but remains popular. If the company stops selling it, customers complain. Mom Wilson's also makes Panhas, *souse, and head cheese. The mart is closed over the summer.*

Neese Country Sausage Company, Inc.
1452 Alamance Church Rd.
Greensboro, NC 27406
(336) 275-9548
Established 1917. Liver pudding, liver mush, and scrapple. The Neese family originally came from Berks County, Pennsylvania.

Orangeburg Sausage Company
597 High St.
Orangeburg, SC 29115
(803) 536-2754
Established 1953. Sells liver mush as Osco brand liver pudding. Also makes souse.

Parks Sausage Company
3330 Henry G. Parks Jr. Circle
Baltimore, MD 21215
(410) 664-5050
Established 1951.

Peters Brothers Meat Market, Inc.
65 Penn St.
Lenhartsville, PA 19534
(610) 562-2231
*Established 1940. Makes scrapple, liver pudding in
casings, and pot pudding in pans.*

Philadelphia Fevre Steak and Hoagie Shop
2332 E. Madison St.
Seattle, WA 98112
*A high altar for fans of all things Philadelphia, including a good
supply of scrapple. Website: www.phillysteakshop.com.*

R & R Provision Company
1240 Pine St.
Easton, PA 18042-4167
(610) 258-5366
Established 1934. Makes scrapple for regional retailers.

Rapa Scrapple Company (Ralph & Paul Adams, Inc.)
Market St. & Railroad Ave.
Bridgeville, DE 19933
(800) 338-4727
*Established 1926. Purchased in 1981 as a division of Jones Dairy
Farm of Fort Atkinson, Wisconsin. Packages wholesale scrapple
under several labels and a variety of flavors, including beef, bacon,
and hot-and-spicy. Online sales at www.rapascrapple.com.*

Ratchford's Market, Inc.
204 Magnolia Place
Guyton, GA 31312
(912) 772-3535
*Established 1916. Most of the business is devoted to a special
"hot meat" processed sausage, but liver pudding is also an
important sideline—and a local delicacy.*

Reading Terminal Market
12th and Arch Streets
Philadelphia, PA 19107
Established 1892. Four merchants at the market sell scrapple,
although they do not necessarily make it themselves. These
retailers are Dutch Country Meats, (215) 922-5842; L. Halteman
Family—Country Foods, (215) 925-3206; Martin's Meats, (215)
629-1193; and Harry Ochs & Son, (215) 922-0303.

Rizer Pork and Produce
2398 Confederate Highway
Lodge, SC 29082
(843) 866-2645
Established 2000. Makes country pork pudding.

Schneck's Meats
173 Hickory Rd.
Pine Grove, PA 17963
(570) 345-3377
Established 1938.

S. Clyde Weaver
5253 Main St.
East Petersburg, PA 17520
(888) 932-8374
Established 1920. Sells scrapple and pan pudding. Online
ordering at www.sclydeweaver.com.

Seltzer's Smokehouse Meats
230 N. College St.
Palmyra, PA 17078
(800) 353-2244
Established 1902. Online ordering at www.seltzersbologna.com.

Shuff's Meat Market
12247 Baugher Rd.
Thurmont, MD 21788
(301) 271-2231
Established 1956. Makes old-style scrapple and liver pudding.
Website: www.areaguides.com/shuffmeat.

Starliper's Butchering Shop
13783 Buchanan Trl. W.
Mercersburg, PA 17236
(717) 328-5125
Established 1988. Custom butchering; makes scrapple to order.

Steely Meats
54 Mount Pleasant Rd.
Fayetteville, PA 17222-9317
(717) 352-3272
Established 1973. Makes scrapple under the label "ponhoss with meat," as well as pan pudding.

Stoltzfus Meats
P.O. Box 447
Intercourse, PA 17534-0447
(800) 347-6653
Established 1958. Online ordering at www.stoltzfusmeats.com.

Thurn's Specialty Meats, Inc.
530 Greenlawn Ave.
Columbus, OH 43223
(614) 443-1449
Established 1886. Packages and distributes scrapple locally.

Troutman Brothers Meats
High Road
Klingerstown, PA 17941
(570) 425-2341
Established 1929. Makes scrapple in the winter only.

Weaver's (Daniel Weaver Bologna Company)
15th Ave. & Weavertown Rd.
Lebanon, PA 17042
(717) 274-6100
Established 1885. Distributes scrapple under Strode's label. Strode's was purchased by Weaver's in 1983 and is now a division of the company. Online ordering at www.lebanon-bologna.com.

Weavers of Wellsville
47 North St.
Wellsville, PA 17365-0066
(717) 432-4146
Established 1889.

Wehry Farms T T & A Quality Meats
R.D. 1, Box 170
Klingerstown, PA 17941
(570) 425-3685
Established 1999. Formerly owned by Kenneth L. Boyer, who established the firm in 1960. Produces scrapple under the commercial name Snow Creek Brand Ponhaus.

Wightman Farms
111 Mt. Kemble Rd.
Morristown, NJ 07960
(973) 425-0840
Established 1922. Online ordering at www.wightmansfarms.com.

Williams Brothers Meat Market
607 W. Fifth St.
Washington, MO 63090
(636) 239-2183
Established 1982. Distributes scrapple under the label Washington Meats. Online ordering at www.justabouttown.com.

German Museums Relevant to Panhas and Goetta

Check the websites for updated hours and entrance fees as well as current exhibits and special events. Most of the websites are multi-lingual. Click on the British or American flag for English.

Bauernhaus-Museum
Dornberger Strasse 82
33617 Bielefeld, Germany
Website: www.bielefeld.de/en/attractions/museums
Features a 1590 farmhouse, a 1686 post mill, a 1764 bakehouse, and various other buildings, focusing on the economic and social system of the region.

Landesmuseum für Kunst und Kulturgeschichte Oldenburg
Schlossplatz 26
26122 Oldenburg, Germany
Website: www.landesmuseum-oldenburg.de
Historical museum in an old palace, focusing on the cultural
history of the Oldenburg region.

Museumsdorf Cloppenburg
Niederrheinisches Freilichtmuseum
Postfach 1344
49661 Cloppenburg, Germany
Website: www.museumsdorf.de
An open-air village. Pottery, weaving, and culinary activities.

Rheinisches Freilichtmuseum für Volkskunde—Kommern
Auf dem Kahlenbusch
53894 Mechernich-Kommern, Germany
Website: www.kommern.de
A scenic village near Cologne assembled from old buildings.
Particular emphasis is placed on daily life and traditional
handcrafts, including a brewery.

Westfälisches Freilichtmuseum Detmold
Krummes Haus
32760 Detmold, Germany
Website: www.fm-detmold@lwl.org
A village assembled from old buildings. Numerous craft
demonstrations, including food preparation.

Westfälisches Freilichtmuseum Hagen
Mäckingerbach
58091 Hagen, Germany
Website: www.freilichtmuseum-hagen.de
Specializes in handcrafts and preindustrial technologies.

NOTES

1. Pierre-Yves Lambert, *La langue gauloise* (Paris, 1997), 57.

2. Christian Holliger, *Culinaria Romana* (Brugg, 1983), 47.

3. Umberto Albarella and Dale Serjeantson, "A Passion for Pork: Meat Consumption at the British Late Neolithic Site of Durrington Walls," in *Consuming Passions and Patterns of Consumption,* Preston Miracle and Nicky Milner, eds. (Cambridge, England, 2002), 33–49.

4. James MacKillop, *Dictionary of Celtic Mythology* (Oxford, 1998), 40–41.

5. Lambert (1997), 189. For the botanical data, refer to Peter Hanelt, *Mansfeld's Encyclopedia of Agricultural and Horticultural Crops* (Berlin, 2001), vol. 4, 1884.

6. Mary Ella Milham, ed., *Apicii Decem Libri qui Dicuntur De Re Coquinaria* (Leipzig, 1969), 54.

7. Interview with Maja Godina-Golija, Basel, Switzerland, September 30, 2002. Dr. Godina-Golija is a specialist in Slovenian food history who lives in Ljubljana. She has published numerous articles on this subject.

8. The recipe was published by Willy Louis Braekman, "En nieuw Zuidnederlands kookboek uit de vijftiende eeuw," in *Scripta: Medieval and Renaissance Texts and Studies 17* (Brussels, 1986), 121, recipe no. 326. This transcription was kindly provided by Dr. Johanna Maria Van Winter, University of Utrecht, Netherlands.

9. John M. Klassen, *Letters of the Rožmberk Sisters* (Cambridge, 2001), 83. Anézka wrote to her brother that she had made sausage

from her own pigs, "which has already been boiled." She was probably referring to blood sausage. In *Metzelsupp* fashion, she sent her brother a gift of sausages along with the letter.

10. Kartl Schmidthaus, "Kleine Beiträge aus Berichten der Archives für westfälische Volkskunde, Münster. Essen und Trinken" [Little Contributions Drawn from the Reports of the Archive for Westphalian Popular Culture, Munster. Eating and Drinking], *Rheinish-westfälische Zeitschrift für Volkskunde* 11:1–4 (1964), 89–102.

11. Georg Bachem, *Keltoromansch im Gau Köln-Aachen* [The Celto-Roman Language in the Cologne-Aachen Region] (Cologne, 1968), 160.

12. Gisela Allkemper and Annelene von der Haar, *Das Kochbuch aus dem Münsterland* [Cookbook from the Münster Region] (Münster, 1976), 27.

13. Dorothea Schneider, "Hunsrücker Nahrungsgewohnheiten" [Everyday Diet in Hunsrück], *Mainzer Kleine Schriftten zur Volkskultur* 12 (1997), 128.

14. Udelgard Körber-Grohne, *Nutzpflanzen in Deutschland* [The Cultivated Plants of Germany] (Stuttgart, 1988), 339–49.

15. O. Schell, "Etwas vom Essen und Trinken im Bergischen" [Tidbits on Eating and Drinking in the Berg Region], *Zeitschrift des Vereins für rheinische und westfälische Volkskunde* 15 (1918), 87.

16. *American Husbandry* (London, 1775), vol. 1, 100, 135.

17. Peter Veltman, "Dutch Survivals in Holland, Michigan," *American Speech* (February 1940), 80–83.

18. James Lemon, *The Best Poor Man's Country* (Baltimore, 1972), 152, 155, 157, 171, 172.

19. Henry Melchior Muhlenberg, *Journals* (Phildelphia, 1958), vol. 3, 613.

20. Johann Noever, "Lebensmittel und Ernährung in volkskundlicher Sicht" [Food and Diet from a Folk Cultural View], *Die Heimat: Zeitschrift für nierderrheinische Heimatpflege* 27 (1956), 19.

21. Job Roberts, *The Pennsylvania Farmer* (Philadelphia, 1804), 173.

22. William Drowns, *The Farmer's Guide* (Providence, RI, 1824), 99.

23. Richard Parkinson, *Tour in America in 1798, 1799, and 1800* (London, 1805), vol. 1, 290–91.

24. *Pioneer Days in the Southwest* (Guthrie, OK, 1909), 142.

25. Paul Sartori, *Westfälische Volkskunde* [Westphalian Folk Culture] (Leipzig, 1929), 108. Also refer to his extensive footnotes on page 192.

26. Ernst Meier, "Gewerksausdrücke des Schlachters in Westfalen" [Workday Expressions of the Butchers in Westphalia], *Jahresbericht des historischen Vereins für die Grafschaft Ravensberg zu Bielefeld* 29 (1915), 1–69.

27. Rebecca Rhoads, "Diary" (Philadelphia, 1831–57). The entry is dated "12th month 1832, 28th."

28. Philadelphia butchers were organized into associations similar to guilds, which were broken down into beef butchers, calf butchers, sheep butchers, and hog butchers. There was also a Butcher's Hide and Tallow Association and a group called Knights of the Cleaver. Quakers were not permitted to belong to organizations that required oaths.

29. George Bates, *A Biography of Deceased Butchers* (Philadelphia, 1877), 37.

30. For a full discussion and translation of *Die Geschickte Hausfrau,* refer to William Woys Weaver, *Sauerkraut Yankees* (Mechanicsburg, PA, 2002).

31. Aunt Mary (pseudonym), *The Philadelphia Housewife* (Philadelphia, 1855), 41.

32. Thomas DeVoe, *The Market Assistant* (New York, 1866), 96.

33. Hannah Widdifield, *Widdifield's New Cook Book* (Philadelphia, 1856), 183.

34. Elizabeth Lea, *Domestic Cookery* (Baltimore, 1851), 169.

35. Phebe Earle Gibbons, *The Pennsylvania Dutch and Other Essays* (Philadelphia, 1872), 40.

36. DeVoe (1866), 104.

37. Robert Schneider, "Country Butcher: An Interview with Newton Bachman," *Pennsylvania Folklife* 20:4 (Summer 1971), 21.

38. Henry Hartshorne, *Household Cyclopedia of General Information* (Philadelphia, 1871), 191.

39. Samuel Haldeman, *Pennsylvania Dutch* (London, 1872), 20.

40. Edward Rauch, *Rauch's Pennsylvania Dutch Hand-Book* (Mauch Chunk, 1879), 128.

41. For material on the growth of the north German dairy industry, refer to Helmut Ottenjann and Karl-Heinz Ziessow, eds., *Die Milch* [Milk] (Cloppenburg, 1996).

42. Interview with Grace Hickman Weaver (1900–97), July 20, 1983. Her father turned over the Pocopson business to a son in 1912 and moved to West Chester, Pennsylvania, where he maintained a butcher shop on Market Street for several years.

43. Charles Dickens, *American Notes* (London, c. 1880), 69. The late Arthur D. Graeff also arrived at the conclusion that the "black pudding" was scrapple because true black pudding (blood pudding) was not eaten for breakfast in Pennsylvania. It rarely shows up in historical Pennsylvania menus except in connection with German wine taverns and brewery pubs. See Arthur D. Graeff, "Dickens and Panhaas," *Morning Call* (Allentown, PA), September 28, 1946.

44. *Practical Housekeeping* (Minneapolis, 1884), 408, 411, 413. At the end of the recipe on page 411, the editors added this note: "Those who are unacquainted with this dish, and many of our readers are, should give it a trial."

45. *Cooking Club Magazine* (February 1906), 65.

46. Sarah Tyson Rorer, *Recipes Used in Illinois Corn Exhibit Model Kitchen* (Philadelphia, 1893). The scrapple recipe appears on page 11.

47. Emma Weigley, *Sarah Tyson Rorer* (Philadelphia, 1977), 95.

48. *Table Talk* 9:6 (June 1894), 95.

49. *Table Talk's Cook Book* (Philadelphia, 1897), 107.

50. "Turkey Scrapple," *American Cooking* 45:7 (February 1941), 423.

51. Raven I. McDavid, "Grist for the Atlas Mill," *American Speech* (April 1949), 112–14.

52. C. I. Macafee, *A Concise Ulster Dictionary* (Oxford, 1996), 290.

53. Frauen Verein Society of Trinity Lutheran Church, *Cook Book* (Pottsville, PA, c. 1925), 11. The recipe is doubly interesting, as it represents a dish eaten by black coal-mining families living in the Pottsville area.

54. Stephenson Mission Band, *Abingdon Recipes* (Bristol, TN, 1910), 15.

55. John Nott, *Cooks and Confectioners Dictionary* (London, 1726), 234.

56. My special thanks to James Mixson, grandson of Onnie Lee Smoak, who has permitted me to publish this material. The actual recipe is available on Mixson's website at www.mixson.org.

57. Horace Kephart, *Our Southern Highlanders* (Knoxville, TN, 1980), 366–67.

58. *Pioneer Days in the Southwest* (Guthrie, OK, 1909), 252–53.

59. Sherman Kuhn, *Middle English Dictionary* (Ann Arbor, 1983), vol. P, part 2, 1171.

60. For example, see James Villas, *Stews, Bogs & Burgoos* (New York, 1997). No history, but many recipes.

61. Interview, Evelina Polk, December 28, 2002. Polk is part Cherokee and part African-American.

62. Dan Looker, "Pig," *Encyclopedia of Food and Culture* (New York, 2002), vol. 3, 75.

63. Evan Jones, *American Food* (New York, 1975), 68.

64. For an in-depth look at the Alice Waters phenomenon, refer to Patric Kuh, *The Last Days of Haute Cuisine* (New York, 2001), 133–48.

65. Bland Johaneson, *Victualary among the Pennsylvania Germans* (Cedar Rapids, IA, 1928), 5–6.

66. Tom Scocca, "You Gonna Eat That?" *Baltimore Citypaper,* February 23–29, 2000.

67. Charles Goodnight et al., *Pioneer Days in the Southwest* (Guthrie, OK, 1909), 72.

68. Women's Club of Bethlehem, *Recipes and Menus* (Bethlehem, PA, 1921), 183.

69. Maria Dembinska, *Food and Drink in Medieval Poland* (Philadelphia, 1999), 112.

70. Mary Gunderson, *The Food Journal of Lewis and Clark* (Yankton, SD, 2003), 22.

71. Interview with Margaret Lauterbach, Boise, Idaho, January 11, 2001.

ANNOTATED BIBLIOGRAPHY

References to scrapple are so numerous that it is impossible to compile a full list of the publications dealing with it. The following bibliography is therefore highly selective. It includes both the works cited in the text as well as representative sources treating some aspect of scrapple or its preparation.

Books and Journal Articles

Aabel, Marie. *Die Schlachtpartie im Hause* [Butchering at Home]. Gotha: Paul Hartung, 1889. The title implies a festive atmosphere. The recipes are directed at urban middle-class readers who have ready access to high-class butchers.

Adam, Hans Karl. *German Cookery.* Cleveland: World Publishing Company, 1967. Published a Westphalian recipe for *Panhas* employing diced bacon, pork blood, and buckwheat flour.

Alberella, Umberto, and Dale Serjeantson, "A Passion for Pork: Meat Consumption at the British Late Neolithic Site of Durrington Walls." In *Consuming Passions and Patterns of Consumption,* edited by Preston Miracle and Nicky Milner, 33–49. Cambridge: McDonald Institute for Archeological Research, 2002. The authors detect evidence of seasonal special ritual killing of pigs based on bone remains.

Allkemper, Gisela, and Annelene von der Haar. *Das Kochbuch aus dem Münsterland* [Cookbook from the Münster Region]. Münster: W.

Hölker, 1976. Most of the local dishes have been improved to appeal to popular taste.

American Husbandry. London: J. Bew, 1775. A large, two-volume work written anonymously by an American. The author was either John Mitchell (1711–68) or Arthur Young (1741–1820), according to research in the 1930s. Much on buckwheat.

André, Jacques, trans. and ed. *L'Art culinaire.* Paris: Société D'Édition "Les Belles Lettres," 1987. Useful notes on the meat and sausage dishes.

Apicius. See listings under André and Milham.

Arnold, Samuel. *Eating Up the Santa Fe Trail.* Niwot, CO: University Press of Colorado, 1990.

Ashcom, B. B. "Notes on the Language of the Bedford, Pennsylvania, Subarea." *American Speech* (December 1953), 241–55.

Aubin, Hermann, Theodor Frings, and Josef Müller. *Kulturström-mungen und Kulturprovinzen in dem Rheinland: Geschichte, Sprache, Volkskunde* [Cultural Currents and Provinces in the Rhineland: History, Language, and Folk Culture]. Cologne: L. Röhrscheid, 1926. Deals primarily with linguistic subregions; useful to understanding the great variation in regional terms for *Panhas.*

Aunt Mary (pseudonym). *The Philadelphia Housewife.* Philadelphia: J. B. Lippincott & Co., 1855.

Bachem, Georg Andreas. *Keltoromanisch im Gau Köln-Aachen* [The Celto-Roman Language in the Cologne-Aachen Region]. Cologne: Landschaftsverband Rheinland, 1968. The author presumed (incorrectly) that *pannas* derived from *painnse,* the Gaulish word for tripe.

Bates, George. *A Biography of Deceased Butchers.* Philadelphia: Thomas E. Bagg, 1877.

Birlinger, Anton. "Älteres Küchen- und Kellerdeutsch" [Old-Time Kitchen-and-Cellar German]. *Alemannia* 18 (1890), 244–67. Odd culinary and food storage terms from the Middle Ages to the early eighteenth century.

Boekenoogen, G. J., and J. H. van Lessen, eds. *Woordenboeck der Ned-erlandsche Taal* [Dictionary of the Dutch Language]. 's-Graven-hage: Martinus Nijhoff/Leiden: A. W. Sijthoff's Uitg. MüN. V., 1931.

Bosson, M. B. *Aunt Mena's Recipe Book.* Philadelphia: National Baptist, 1888. Sold for the benefit of a Baptist orphanage in the Angora section of Philadelphia. The recipe for Kane City scrapple employs the head and calls for both cornmeal and buckwheat as thickeners.

Campbell, C. G. "Buckwheat *Fagopyrum.*" In *Evolution of Plant Crops,* 235–37, edited by N. W. Simmonds. London: Longman, 1976.

Carnacina, Luigi, and Vincenzo Buonassisi, eds. *Il Libro della Polenta* [The Book of Polenta]. Florence: Aldo Martello—Giunti Editore, 1974. A wide-ranging survey of cornmeal-based porridges, including black polenta made with the addition of buckwheat.

Casparek, Gustav. *Das Kochbuch aus dem Rheinland* [Cookbook from the Rhineland]. Münster: Wolfgang Hölker, 1985. Recipes and comments on *Panhas.*

Christmann, Ernst, Julius Krämer, and Josef Schwing, eds. *Pfälzisches Wörterbuch* [Dictionary of Palatine German]. Wiesbaden: Franz Steiner Verlag, 1965.

Collen, Jaques. *Lekker Limburg: Historische Recepten met Hedendaagse Ingrediënten* [Limburg Delicacies: Historical Recipes with Modern Ingredients]. Antwerp: Uitgeverij CODA, 1994.

Colonna, Francesco. *Hypnerotomachie, ou discourse du songe de Poliphile* [Hypnerotomachie, or Discourse on the Song of Poliphilius]. Paris: I. Keruer, 1561. One of the most famous editions of this book appeared in 1499.

Davidis, Henrietta. *Praktisches Kochbuch für die gewöhnliche und feinere Küche* [Practical Cookbook for Common and Refined Kitchens]. Bielefeld: Velhagen und Klasing, 1847. The first edition, under a different title, was published at Osnabrück in 1845. Ironically, it took Davidis eight years to find a publisher for her now-famous work.

———. *Praktisches Kochbuch für die Deutschen in Amerika* [Practical Cookbook for Germans in America]. Milwaukee: George Brumder, 1879. This book was published after the death of Davidis and represented a light reworking of her original cookbook. There were several later American editions.

Dembinska, Maria. *Food and Drink in Medieval Poland.* Revised and adapted by William Woys Weaver. Philadelphia: University of Pennsylvania Press, 1999.

DeVoe, Thomas. *The Market Assistant.* New York: Orange Judd & Company, 1866.

Dickens, Charles. *American Notes and Pictures from Italy.* London: Chapman & Hall, c. 1880.

Die bürgerliche Küche oder Anleitung gut, schmackhaft und wohlfeil kochen zu lernen. Vol. 1. *Fleischspeisen.* Urfahr/Linz: Druck und Verlag von Ph. Krauslich, c. 1851. Paperback of forty-eight pages, same size and format as *Die Geschickte Hausfrau.*

Diehl, Lorraine B., and Marianne Hardart. *The Automat: The History, Recipes, and Allure of Horn & Hardart's Masterpiece.* New York: Clarkson Potter, 2002. What Philadelphians praised most about Horn & Hardart was the scrapple. Not a word in this book about scrapple.

Dieffenbach, Victor C. "Butchering Day on the Farm." *Pennsylvania Dutchman* 4:9 (January 1, 1953).

Dirksen, Karl. "Volkskundliches aus Meidrich" [Folk Culture in Meidrich]. *Rheinische Geschichtsblätter* [Rheinland Historical Papers] 1 (1895), 305–19, 336–50, 364–74. A large section on butchering, with comments on *Panhas.*

Drown, William. *Compendium of Agriculture; or, the Farmer's Guide.* Providence, RI: Field & Maxcy, 1824.

Duden. Das grosse Wörterbuch der deutschen Sprache [Duden. The Large Dictionary of the German Language]. Mannheim/Leipzig/Wien/Zürich: Dudenverlag, 1999. *Panhas* is discussed in vol. 6:2842. Variant spellings are *Pannhass* and *Pannharst.*

Durman, Louise. "Leftover Baked Goods Spirited into Rum Cake." *Knoxville News-Sentinel* (February 6, 2002). The second part of this article deals with two scrapple recipes, one served cold like pâté, the other made with milk.

Easton, Alice. *Recipes and Menus for Restaurant Profit.* Stamford, CT: Dahls, 1940. Features an often-reprinted recipe for turkey scrapple using leftovers from Thanksgiving or Christmas turkeys.

Elkin, James. *Snyder Family of Dora, Pennsylvania.* Zanesville, OH: Privately printed, 1999. A cookbook that mixes genealogy and cookery. Contains a recipe for scrapple made from liverwurst.

Ellis, Susan J. "Traditional Food in the Commercial Market: The History of Pennsylvania Scrapple." *Pennsylvania Folklife* 22:3 (Spring 1973), 10–21. A well-researched look at the way in which scrapple has been sold in farm markets and butcher shops.

Elpers, Max. "Hausschlachtung" [Home Butchering]. In *Bäuerliche und Handwerkliche Arbeitsgeräte in Westfalen* [Farm and Handcraft Tools in Westphalia], edited by Hinrich Siuts, 183–195. Münster, 1982. Includes detailed drawings of all the traditional butchering utensils.

Enterprise Manufacturing Company. *Illustrated Catalogue.* Philadelphia: Enterprise ManufacturingCompany, 1889. Contains meat grinders specifically used for scrapple.

Exner, Eva. *Rheinisch-Westfälische Spezialitäten* [Rhineland and Westphalian Specialties]. Munich: Heyne Verlag, 1971.

Farwell, Harold F. *Smoky Mountain Voices: A Lexicon of Southern Appalachian Speech.* Lexington, KY: University Press of Kentucky, 1993.

Frauen Verein Society, Trinity Lutheran Church. *Cook Book.* Pottsville, PA: Privately printed, c. 1925.

Frederick, J. George. *Cooking as Men Like It.* New York: Business Bourse, 1930. An anecdotal discourse that attempts at philosophy. Frederick waxes nostalgic over scrapple, which he suggests grilling or baking rather than frying.

———. *The Pennsylvania Dutch and Their Cookery.* New York: Business Bourse, 1935. An entire chapter is devoted to scrapple and numerous ways of preparing it.

Fulton, A. W. *Home Pork Making.* New York: Orange Judd, 1900. Features a traditional recipe for scrapple using cornmeal, but also discusses buckwheat thickening and various serving suggestions.

Gaertner, Pierre, and Robert Frédérick. *The Cuisine of Alsace.* New York: Barron's, 1981.

Garavini, Daniela. *Pigs and Pork: History, Folklore, Ancient Recipes.* Cologne: Könemann, 1996.

Gehman, Richard. *The Sausage Book.* Englewood Cliffs, NJ: Prentice-Hall, 1969. The author refers to scrapple as an abomination but publishes two recipes, one of them allegedly Shaker. This is a book that cannot be taken seriously.

Gibbons, Phebe Earle. *Pennsylvania Dutch and Other Essays.* Mechanicsburg, PA: Stackpole Books, 2001. Reprint of the 1882 Philadelphia edition, with a new introduction by Don Yoder.

Gibson, Josephine. *Tested Recipes and Planned Menus Prepared for Arbogast & Bastian Co.* Allentown, PA: Arbogast & Bastian, c. 1930.

Giger, Mrs. Frederick Sidney. *Colonial Receipt Book.* Philadelphia: John C. Winston, 1907. A fund-raiser for the University of Pennsylvania Hospital. An heirloom recipe for scrapple was submitted from Capon Springs, West Virginia.

Goodnight, Charles, Emanuel Dubbs, John A. Hart, et al. *Pioneer Days in the Southwest from 1850 to 1879.* Guthrie, OK: State Capital, 1909.

Graham, James. *Jim Graham's Farm Family Cookbook for City Folks.* Raleigh: North Carolina Agricultural Foundation, North Carolina State University, 2002.

Gunderson, Mary. *The Food Journal of Lewis and Clark: Recipes for an Expedition.* Yankton, SD: History Cooks, 2003. Contains a recipe for scrapple.

Haar, Annelene von der. *Das Kochbuch aus Ostfriesland* [The Cookbook from East Friesland]. Münster: W. Hölker, 1975.

Haldeman, Samuel S. *Pennsylvania Dutch: A Dialect of South German with an Infusion of English.* London: Trübner & Co., 1872. A university professor, Haldeman attempted to define scrapple, noting that the terms *Panhas* and *scrapple* are used conjointly.

Hanelt, Peter, ed. *Mansfeld's Encyclopedia of Agricultural and Horticultural Crops.* Berlin: Springer Verlag, 2001. 6 vols. Contains material on buckwheat and an extensive buckwheat bibliography.

Hark, Ann, and Preston A. Barba. *Pennsylvania German Cookery.* Allentown, PA: Schlechter's, 1950. Provides a highly conjectural etymology of the word *Panhas* and tries to create a distinction between it and scrapple.

Hartshorne, Henry. *The Household Cyclopedia of General Information.* Philadelphia: T. Ellwood Zell; Pittsfield, MA: J. Brainard Clarke, 1871.

Hasson, Nancy. "Foods of Butchering." *Goschenhoppen Region* 1:3 (1969), 14–19. Contains a recipe for scrapple from the Brunk family of Royersford, Pennsylvania.

Heath, Ambrose. *Pig Curing and Cooking.* London: Faber, 1952.

Hebbring, Judi, ed. *Buffalo Cook Book.* Fort Pierre, SD: National Buffalo Association, 1989.

Heller, B., & Company. *Secrets of Meat Curing and Sausage Making.* Chicago: B. Heller & Company, 1908. Contains a recipe for scrapple using Bull-Meat-Brand flour.

Hieatt, Constance, and Sharon Butler. *Curye on Inglysch.* Oxford: Oxford University Press, 1985. Contains many references to medieval haslet recipes and pork puddings.

Hill, Annabella P. *Mrs. Hill's New Cook Book.* New York: Carleton, 1872. Hill was from western Georgia, where she wrote this Reconstruction cookbook.

Holliger, Christian. *Culinaria Romana.* Brugg: Vindonissa Museum, 1983. This is a catalog for an exhibit on Roman artifacts from ancient Vindonissa in Switzerland.

Holthof, Ludwig. "Rheinische Küche und rheinische Küchenspezialitäten" [The Rhineland Kitchen and Culinary Specialties]. *Kochkunst*

[Cookery Magazine] 4 Jg. (1902), 189–92. Gastronomic observations on the high-style cuisine of the Rhineland, with critical comments about the lack of authenticity in the "compromise cookery" of hotels and restaurants, especially *die blonde Küche* (white sauce cuisine).

Hundhausen, Emil. "Alter Haushaltrezepte (1682) und Konservierungsmethoden" [Old Housekeeping Recipes (1682) and Food Preservation Methods]. *Rheinische Heimatpflege* [Preservation of Rhineland Regional Culture] 3 (1966), 305–20. Recipes from the Urbarium (ground rent account book) of the St. Laurentius (Catholic) Church at Dattenfeld-an-der-Sieg.

Hutchison, Ruth. *The Pennsylvania Dutch Cook Book.* New York: Harper & Brothers, 1948. Insightful comments on the proper way to make scrapple, along with a recipe that identifies the dish as Pennsylvania Dutch *Panhas.*

James, Pamela. "The American Breakfast, Circa 1873–1973." *Pennsylvania Folklife* 24:2 (Winter 1974–75), 40–48.

James, Virginia E. *Mother James' Key to Good Cooking.* New York: N. D. Thompson, 1892.

Johaneson, Bland. *Victualary among the Pennsylvania Germans.* Cedar Rapids, IA: Torch Press, 1928.

Johnson, Cuthbert W. *The Farmer's Encyclopaedia and Dictionary of Rural Affairs.* Edited by Gouverneur Emerson. Philadelphia: Carey and Hart, 1844. An Americanized edition of an old standard English work.

Johnson, Helen Louise. *The Enterprising Housekeeper.* Philadelphia: Enterprise Manufacturing Company, 1896. Contains a scrapple recipe developed for the Enterprise meat grinders.

Jones, Evan. *American Food.* New York: E. P. Dutton, 1975.

Kephart, Horace. *Our Southern Highlanders.* New York: Macmillan Co., 1922. This book first appeared in 1913. Page references are to the University of Tennessee Press reprint edition of 1980.

Ketchum, Richard, et al. *The American Heritage Cookbook.* New York: American Heritage Publishing Co., 1964. Scrapple is singled out as a regional food representative of the Pennsylvania Dutch.

Klassen, John M., ed. *The Letters of the Rožmberk Sisters: Noble Women in Fifteenth-Century Bohemia.* Cambridge: D. S. Brewer, 2001.

Körber-Grohne, Udelgard. *Nutzpflanzen in Deutschland* [The Cultivated Plants of Germany]. Stuttgart: Konrad Theiss, 1988. Extensive treatment of buckwheat and its history. Mentions *Panhass.*

Kramer, Karl-Sigismund. *Fränkische Alltagsleben um 1500* [Daily Life in Franconia Around 1500]. Würzburg: Echter, 1985.

Kuh, Patric. *The Last Days of Haute Cuisine: America's Culinary Revolution.* New York: Viking, 2001.

Ladies' Sewing Society. *Catskill Cook Book.* Catskill, NY: Ladies' Sewing Society of St. Luke's Church, 1911.

Lambert, Marcus. *A Dictionary of the Non-English Words of the Pennsylvania-German Dialect.* Lancaster, PA: Pennsylvania German Society, 1924. Unsuccessfully attempts to unlock the linguistic origin of *Panhas*, but recognizes the dish as a distinctively regional preparation with European antecedents.

Lambert, Pierre-Yves. *La langue gauloise* [The Gaulish Language]. Paris: Editions Errance, 1997. Contains new material on the linguistic and conceptual origins of *pannas* and related butchering preparations.

Latham, R. E. *Revised Medieval Latin Word-List.* London: British Academy, 1965.

Lea, Elizabeth Ellicott. *Domestic Cookery.* Baltimore: Cushings and Bailey, 1851.

Lemon, James T. *The Best Poor Man's Country: A Geographical Study of Early Southeastern Pennsylvania.* Baltimore: Johns Hopkins, 1972.

Leslie, Eliza. *Directions for Cookery.* Philadelphia: Carey & Hart, 1848. This book was first issued in 1837.

Lewis, Robert E., and John Reidy. *Middle English Dictionary.* Ann Arbor: University of Michigan Press, 1986.

Lissner, Erich. *Wurstologie oder Es geht um die Wurst. Eine Monographie über die Wurst* [Sausage-ology or Everything to Do with Sausage]. Wiesbaden-Biebrich: Kalle & Co., 1939. Issued as an amusing Christmas gift for friends of the firm Kalle & Company. Now a popular collector's item.

Lobel, Leon, and Stanley Lobel. *All about Meat.* New York: Harcourt Brace Jovanovich, 1975. Discusses scrapple and even provides directions for making it. The Lobels were well-known butchers on Madison Avenue in New York.

Long, Amos. "Pig Pens and Piglore." *Pennsylvania Folklife* 19:2 (Winter 1970–71), 19–32.

Looker, Dan. "Pig." *Encyclopedia of Food and Culture.* New York: Charles Scribner's, 2002, vol. 3, 74–81.

Macafee, C. I. *A Concise Ulster Dictionary.* Oxford: Oxford University Press, 1996.

Mackenzie's Five Thousand Receipts. Philadelphia: James Kay, 1830.

Mackenzie's Ten Thousand Receipts. Philadelphia: T. Ellwood Zell, 1867. A revised edition by a well-known Quaker publisher. Includes a recipe for scrapple reproduced from Elizabeth Lea's *Domestic Cookery.*

MacKillop, James. *Dictionary of Celtic Mythology.* Oxford: Oxford University Press, 1998.

Maier, Bernhard. *Die Religion der Kelten* [The Religion of the Celts]. Munich: C. H. Beck, 2001.

Maurizio, Adamo. *Getreide, Mehl und Brot* [Grain, Flour and Bread]. Berlin: Parey, 1903.

McDavid, Raven I. "Grist for the Atlas Mill." *American Speech* (April 1949), 105–14.

Meier, Ernst. "Gewerksausdrücke des Schlachters in Westfalen mit besonderer Berücksichtigung Ravensbergs" [Workday Expressions of the Butchers in Westphalia with Particular Consideration for Ravensberg]. *Jahresbericht des historischen Vereins für die Grafschaft Ravensberg zu Bielefeld* [Annual Report for the Historical Society of the County of Ravensberg at Bielefeld] 29 (1915), 1–69.

Méniel, Patrice. *Les gauloise et les animaux.* Paris: Editions Errance, 2001. Considerable material on Gaulish butchering practices based on archeological finds. Various cuts of pork are discussed on page 21.

Milham, Mary Ella, ed. *Apicii Decem Libri Qui Dicuntur De Re Coquinaria.* Leipzig: B. G. Teubner, 1969.

Muhlenberg, Henry Melchior. *The Journals of Henry Melchior Muhlenberg.* Translated by Theodore Tappert and John Doberstein. Philadelphia: Evangelical Lutheran Ministerium, 1942–58. 3 vols.

Müller, Josef, ed. *Rheinisches Wörterbuch* [Dictionary of Lower Rhineland German]. Berlin: Erika Klopp Verlag, 1944.

Müller-Lubitz, Anna. *Die Schlachtküche in 100 Erprobten Rezepten* [Butchering Cookery in 100 Tested Recipes]. Leipzig: Jaeger'sche Verlagsbuchhandlung, 1902. This is part of a series intended for home cooks.

Münster, W. D. von. *Westfälisches Koch- und Haushaltungsbuch* [Westphalian Book of Cookery and Housekeeping]. Münster: Coppenrath, 1824. The author of this work ("W. D.") has not been identified.

Myers, Ella E. *The Centennial Cook Book and General Guide.* Philadelphia: J. B. Myers, 1876. Compiled and sold to visitors as a memento of the Centennial Exposition held that year in Philadelphia.

Neil, Marion Harris. *The Thrift Cook Book.* Philadelphia: David McKay, 1919. Former cooking editor of the *Ladies' Home Journal* provides hints on wartime penny savers, including a recipe for nut scrapple.

Neuer, Gemeinnütziger Pennsylvanischer Calender. Lancaster, PA: John Baer, 1892.

Nicholson, Elizabeth. *The Economical Cook and House-Book.* Philadelphia: Willis P. Hazard, 1857. Nicholson, an Orthodox Quaker, published a recipe for scrapple that may trace to a professional pork butcher.

Niederrheinisches Kochbuch [Lower Rhineland Cookbook]. Düsseldorf: Zehnpfennig & Bartscher, 1777.

Niederrheinisches Kochbuch für den bürgerlichen Haushalt [Lower Rhineland Cookbook for Middle-Class Housekeeping]. Duisburg, Germany: W. Braun, 1975. Reprint of the 1900 edition. This book first appeared in the 1860s as the handiwork of three authors: Louise Apel, Rosalie Gruber, and Bertha Schneider. It was published in many parts of Germany under various titles and does not represent regional cookery.

Niederrheinisches Taschenbuch für die Küche und Haushaltung [Lower Rhineland Pocket-Handbook for Cooking and Housekeeping]. Berlin: Tirtia, 1805. This is listed as the second edition.

Noever, Johann. "Lebensmittel und Ernährung in Volkskundlicher Sicht" [Food and Diet from a Folk-Cultural View]. *Die Heimat. Zeitschrift für nieder-rheinische Heimatpflege* [The Homeland. Journal for the Preservation of Lower Rhineland Regional Culture] 27 Jg. (1956), 8–24. Important historical data on the foods and foodways of Crefeld and neighboring regions.

Nott, John. *Cooks and Confectioners Dictionary.* London: Charles Rivington, 1726.

Ochs, Ernst, Karl F. Müller, and Gerhard Bauer, eds. *Badisches Wörterbuch* [Dictionary of Baden German]. Lahr/Schwarzwald: Moritz Schauenburg, 1975–97. Discusses *Metzelsupp.*

Ottenjann, Helmut, and Karl-Heinz Ziessow, eds. *Die Milch: Geschichte und Zukunft eines Lebensmittels* [Milk: The History and Future of a Food]. Cloppenburg: Museumsdorf Cloppenburg/ Niedersächsisches Freilichtmuseum, 1996. Of particular value are the essays on the industrialization of the north German dairy industry between 1871 and 1914.

Oukah. *The Ultimate Cherokee Cookbook.* Dallas: Triskelion Press, 1995. A recipe for acorn mush provides the basis for a scrapplelike dish that might employ bear or squirrel "meal" (pounded, dried meat).

Owens, Frances. *Mrs. Owens' Cook Book.* Chicago: American Publishing, 1903.

"Panhas." *Cooking Club Magazine* 8:2 (February 1906), 65.

Parkinson, Richard. *Tour in America in 1798, 1799, and 1800.* London: Printed for J. Harding, 1805.

Paul, Sara T. *Cookery from Experience.* Philadelphia: Porter & Coates, 1875. The author includes her own recipe for scrapple, which contains many technical details.

Pen Argyl Milling Company. *Recipes. Pocono Heart of Buckwheat Brand.* Pen Argyl, PA: Penn Argyl Milling Company, c. 1970. Commercial pamphlet containing a recipe for chicken scrapple made with kasha.

Peterson, Hannah Bouvier. *The National Cook Book.* Philadelphia: Childs & Peterson, 1855. The author uses cornmeal exclusively in her scrapple recipe, but does allow for buckwheat. She flours her sliced scrapple before frying it—a smart idea to keep it from falling apart.

"Philadelphia Scrapple." *American Cookery* 41:5 (December 1936), 307–8.

"Philadelphia Scrapple": Whimsical Bits Anent Eccentrics and the City's Oddities. Richmond: Dietz Press, 1956. A compilation by several anonymous authors. In spite of the title, this is not a history of the dish, although an heirloom recipe for scrapple from Chester County, Pennsylvania, does appear in a chapter on food.

Potthoff, Ossip Demetrius. *Illustrierte Geschichte des Deutschen Fleischerhandwerks vom 12. Jahrhundert bis zum Gegenwart* [An Illustrated History of German Butchering Practices from the 12th Century to the Present]. Berlin: Askanischen Verlag, 1927. This deals primarily with urban beef-butchering practices, but includes an extensive bibliography on all types of butchering.

Practical Housekeeping. Minneapolis: Buckeye Publishing Company, 1884. This is a thoroughly revised edition of Estelle Woods Wilcox's *Buckeye Cookery and Practical Housekeeping,* which first appeared in 1877 and became a best-seller.

Prince, J. Dyneley. "The Jersey Dutch Dialect." *Dialect Notes* 3:6 (1910), 459–84.

"Processor Builds on Product Quality and Sports Appeal." *National Provisioner* 192:6 (February 9, 1985), 10–14, 15, 18, 23–24, 26, 28,

30, 35–42. An in-depth look at the mechanization of Kessler's meat business in Lemoyne, Pennsylvania.

Randolph, Mary. *The Virginia House-Wife.* Washington, DC: Davis and Force, 1824.

Rauch, Edward H. *Rauch's Pennsylvania Dutch Hand-Book.* Mauch Chunk, PA: E. H. Rauch, 1879. Defined *Panhas* as scrapple.

Reed, Anna Wetherill. *The Philadelphia Cook Book of Town and Country.* New York: M. Barrows and Company, 1940. The author identifies scrapple as a Pennsylvania Dutch food and includes an old recipe using buckwheat as a thickener.

Roberts, Job. *The Pennsylvania Farmer.* Philadelphia: A. Bartram, 1804. Contains comments on buckwheat but no mention of scrapple.

Rorer, Sarah Tyson. *Recipes Used in Illinois Corn Exhibit Model Kitchen.* Philadelphia: G. H. Buchanan Co., 1893. A fifteen-page pamphlet cookbook handed out at the Columbian Exposition in Chicago. Contains a recipe for Philadelphia scrapple.

———. *World's Fair Souvenir Cook Book.* Philadelphia: Arnold & Co., 1903. Recipes prepared in the Eastern Pavilion at the Louisiana Purchase Exposition held in St. Louis.

[Rundell, Maria]. *A New System of Domestic Cookery.* New York: M'Dermut & D. D. Arden, 1815. This is an American edition of a popular English cookbook.

Sartori, Paul. *Westfälische Volkskunde* [Westphalian Popular Culture]. Leipzig: Quelle & Meyer, 1929. Mentions *Panhas* and has important bibliographic references.

Sauer, Christopher. *Sauer's Herbal Cures: America's First Book of Botanic Healing, 1762–1778.* Translated and edited by William Woys Weaver. New York: Routledge, 2001.

Sauers, Roy W. "Butchering on the Pennsylvania Farm." *Der Reggeboge* 27:2 (1993), 21–28. The author's written reply to a folk-cultural questionnaire published in *Pennsylvania Folklife* (1972).

Scharfenberg, Horst. *Die deutsche Küche* [The German Kitchen]. Bern/Stuttgart: Hallvag, 1980. Contains a number of buckwheat dishes that the author associates with the Lower Rhineland. No discussion of *Panhas.* See next entry.

———. *Schlachtfest* [Butchering Day]. Weil der Stadt: Hädecke, 1985. Contains a recipe for Philadelphia scrapple, as the author describes it, "reimportiert" (reimported) to its original homeland.

Scheichelbauer, Carl, and Franz Giblhauser. *Gastronomisches Lexikon.* Vienna: Selbstverlag C. Scheichelbauer, 1908.

Schell, O. "Etwas vom Essen und Trinken im Bergischen" [Tidbits on Eating and Drinking in the Berg Region]. *Zeitschrift des Vereins für rheinische und westfälische Volkskunde* 15 Jg. (1918), 85–88. Mentions *Panhas* and general eating patterns.

Schmidthaus, Karl. "Kleine Beiträge aus Berichten des Archivs für westfälische Volkskunde, Münster. Essen und Trinken. Der Tageslauf im Haushalt" [Little Contributions Drawn from the Reports of the Archive for Westphalian Popular Culture, Munster. Eating and Drinking. Daily Routine in the Household]. *Rheinisch-westfälische Zeitschrift für Volkskunde* 11:1–4 (Bonn/Münster, 1964), 89–102. This refers to Manuscript Document 1383, collected in 1958 from an elderly informant.

Schneider, Dorothea. "Hunsrücker Nahrungsgewohnheiten" [Everyday Diet in Hunsrück], *Mainzer Kleine Schriften zur Volkskultur* [Mainzer Monographs on Popular Culture] 12 (Mainz, 1997), 126–30.

Schneider, Robert. "Country Butcher: An Interview with Newton Bachman." *Pennsylvania Folklife* 20:4 (Summer 1971), 17–22.

Schürmann, K. *Gastliches Westfalen: Streifzug durch westfälische Gasthäuser* [Westphalian Hospitality: An Excursion through Westphalian Inns]. Dortmund: Eigenverlag, 1957. Deals with the postwar revitalization of the hospitality industry. Several of the inns served local food, including *Panhas*.

Schwabe, Calvin W. *Unmentionable Cuisine.* Charlottesville, VA: University Press of Virginia, 1979. Scrapple is indeed included and compared favorably with ham in terms of fat and protein content.

"Scrapple." *Cooking Club Magazine* 9:1 (January 1907), 11.

Shapiro, Laura. *Perfection Salad: Women and Cooking at the Turn of the Century.* New York: Farrar, Straus and Giroux, 1986.

Shoemaker, Alfred L. *Christmas in Pennsylvania.* Introduction and new foreword and afterword by Don Yoder. Mechanicsburg, PA: Stackpole Books, 1999. New edition of the original Kutztown edition of 1959. Extensive material on the *Metzelsupp* custom.

Simmonds, N. W., ed. *Evolution of Plant Crops.* London: Longman, 1976. Contains material on buckwheat.

Sisters of St. Francis. *Illustriertes, Praktisches Kochbuch für die Bürgerliche und Feinere Küche* [Illustrated, Practical Cookbook for Middle Class and Refined Kitchens]. Maastricht: Cl. Goffin, c. 1905. Contains a recipe for *Panhas* designed for teaching in a cooking school run by the order.

Siuts, Hinrich. *Bäuerliche und handwerkliche Arbeitsgeräte in Westfalen* [Farming and Handcraft Tools in Westphalia]. Münster: Aschendorff, 1982. Richly illustrated. Includes drawings of butchering tools as well as traditional meat-smoking processes.

Smedley, Emma. *Institution Recipes*. Media, PA: Emma Smedley, Publisher, 1904. This book, based on home economics, became a classic of its type and underwent numerous editions until 1940. Smedley was an instructor in dietetics at Johns Hopkins University in Baltimore.

Sparks, Elizabeth Hedgecock. *North Carolina and Old Salem Cookery*. Kernersville, NC: TarPar Ltd., 1980. Recipes for both liver mush and liver pudding.

Stauffer, G. W. "Panhaws." *Pennsylvania Dutchman* 4:14 (April 1953), 4, 11.

St. Paul's P.E. Church. *The Housekeeper's Help: A Collection of Valuable Recipes*. Camden, NJ: Daily Post Printing House, 1886.

Stephenson Mission Band of the Presbyterian Church, Abingdon, Va. *Abingdon Recipes*. Bristol, TN: King Printing, 1910. Contains a recipe for scrapple.

Stillé, Charles J. *Memorial of the Great Central Fair for the U.S. Sanitary Commission*. Philadelphia: United States Sanitary Commission, 1864. Features a lengthy discussion of the Pennsylvania Kitchen and its connection with Pennsylvania Dutch cooking. No mention of scrapple, because the fair took place in early summer when scrapple was out of season.

Stradley, Linda. *I'll Have What They're Having: Legendary Local Cuisine*. Guildford, CT: Three Forks/Falcon Publishing, 2002. Material about and recipe for goetta.

Table Talk Magazine. *Table Talk's Cook Book*. Philadelphia: Table Talk Publishing Company, 1897. Includes a scrapple recipe using a cleaned hog's head, cooked and thickened with yellow cornmeal. Refer to *Table Talk* 11:4 (April 1896), 123.

Teepe-Wurmbach, A. "Kohl-Mus-Kraut. Wort- und sachkundliche Untersuchungen zur nordwest-deutschen Gemüse- und Obstbereitung" [Cabbage-Mush-Herb. Terminology and Artifact Research into Northwest German Vegetable and Fruit Preparation]. *Westfälische Forschungen* 14 (1961), 150–68.

ter Laan, K. *Folkloristisch Woordenbock van Nederland en Vlaams België* [Folklore Dictionary of the Netherlands and Flemish Belgium].

's-Gravenhage/Batavia: G. B. Van Goor Zonen, 1949. Discusses Dutch traditions under the term *balkenbrij* and notes the use of the term *panharst* in parts of the Lower Rhineland.

Thorne, John, and Matt Lewis Thorne. *Serious Pig.* New York: North Point Press, 1996.

Tibbot, S. Minwel. *Welsh Fare: A Selction of Traditional Recipes.* Cardiff: Welsh Folk Museum, 1976. Many recipes similar in concept to liver mush.

"Turkey Scrapple." *American Cookery* 45:7 (February 1941), 423.

U.S. Department of Agriculture. *Slaughtering, Cutting, and Processing Pork on the Farm.* Washington, DC: Government Printing Office, 1967. Farmers' Bulletin no. 2138. Includes recipes for both scrapple and *Panhas,* but in such a way that the reader is led to believe (incorrectly) that the two are entirely different preparations.

Van der Meulen, Hielke. *Traditionele Streekgerechten, Gastronomisch Erfgoed van Nederland* [Traditional Regional Dishes, The Gastronomic Heritage of the Netherlands]. Doetinchem: Elsevier, 1998. Excellent exploration of *balkenbrij* in all of its regional variations.

Veltman, Peter. "Dutch Survivals in Holland, Michigan." *American Speech* (February 1940), 80–83. Refers to the use of *balkenbrij* for scrapple.

Villas, James. *Stews, Bogs & Burgoos.* New York: William Morrow, 1997. Recipes, no history about these various preparations.

Ward, Artemas. *The Grocers' Hand-Book and Directory.* Philadelphia: Philadelphia Grocer Publishing Company, 1886. Contains an entry describing scrapple in very accurate terms.

Watel, Therese. *Die wohlerfahrne westphälische Köchin* [The Experienced Westphalian Cook]. Münster: Wundermann, 1828.

Weaver, William Woys. *Pennsylvania Dutch Country Cooking.* New York: Abbeville, 1993. Contains a family recipe for scrapple and a brief history of the dish.

———. *A Quaker Woman's Cookbook: The Domestic Cookery of Elizabeth Ellicott Lea.* Philadelphia: University of Pennsylvania Press, 1982. Lea's book (published in 1845) was transcribed from a manuscript that she began in 1821. Her sensibly adapted recipe for scrapple is also among the oldest to find its way into print. The editor's glossary provides a short history of the dish, although his understanding of scrapple and its origins has since changed.

————. *Sauerkraut Yankees: Pennsylvania Dutch Food and Foodways.* 2nd ed. Mechanicsburg, PA: Stackpole, 2002. Discusses the history of *Panhas* and scrapple, and includes an old-style butcher's recipe from Elizabeth Nicholson's 1857 cookbook (see Nicholson).

————. *35 Receipts from "The Larder Invaded."* Philadelphia: Library Company of Philadelphia/Historical Society of Pennsylvania, 1986. Includes the recipe for scrapple from Elizabeth Nicholson's cookbook (see Nicholson), along with updated procedures and a woodcut of the haslet.

Weber, Johann Jakob, ed. *Universal-Lexikon der Kochkunst* [Universal Lexicon of Cookery]. 2 vols. Leipzig: J. J. Weber, 1897. Provides a recipe for Westphalian *Panhas* made with beef and pork.

Weigley, Emma Seifrit. *Sarah Tyson Rorer: The Nation's Instructress in Dietetics and Cookery.* Philadelphia: American Philosophical Society, 1977.

Wentworth, Harold. *American Dialect Dictionary.* New York: Thomas Y. Crowell, 1944. Discusses scrapple under the term *pannhas.*

Widdifield, Hannah Hungary. *Widdifield's New Cook Book.* Philadelphia: T. B. Peterson, 1856. Does not discuss scrapple, but includes a recipe for haslet sauce for roast pig. The haslet was a traditional scrapple ingredient.

Wiggins, Francis. *The American Farmer's Instructor.* Philadelphia: Orrin Rogers, 1840.

Wilson, Mary A. *Mrs. Wilson's Cook Book.* Philadelphia: J. B. Lippincott, 1920. Cooking school instructor shows how to combine operations for making head cheese and scrapple.

Women's Club of Bethlehem. *Recipes and Menus.* Bethlehem, PA: Home Economics Committee, 1921.

Women's Institute Library of Cookery: Soup, Meat, Poultry, Game, Fish and Shell Fish. Scranton, PA: Women's Institute of Domestic Arts and Sciences, 1918. Scrapple is treated as equivalent to *Panhas.*

Wright, Joseph. *The English Dialect Dictionary.* London: Henry Frowde/New York: G. P. Putnam, 1902.

Yoder, Don. *Discovering American Folklife: Essays on Folk Culture and the Pennsylvania Dutch.* Mechanicsburg, PA: Stackpole Books, 2001.

————. "Pennsylvanians Called It Mush." *Pennsylvania Folklife* 13:2 (Winter 1962–63), 27–49.

Zender, Mathias. "Kleine Beiträge Eifler Mundart und Dorfleben im 19. Jahrhundert" [Small Contributions on Eifel Dialect and Village

Life in the Nineteenth Century]. *Rheinisch-westfälische Zeitschrift für Volkskunde* 21 Jg. (1974), Heft 1–4, 106–24.

Newspaper Articles

"A. Darlington Strode." *Daily Local News* (West Chester, PA), June 18, 1926.

"A. Darlington Strode of West Chester." *Daily Local News* (West Chester, PA), August 10, 1988.

Behney, J. J. "Die Metzel Soup." *Lebanon Evening Report* (Lebanon, PA), February 5, 1900. A dialect poem about butchering stew written in *Pennsylfaanisch.*

Belk, Jan. "Corriher's Recipe for Success." *Salisbury Post* (Salisbury, NC), March 17, 1991.

Blackwood, Frances. "Scrapple Is a Matter of Pride." *Evening Bulletin* (Philadelphia), March 27, 1961. Includes a good basic recipe.

Cipriano, Ralph. "E. H. Habbersett 3rd; Firm Made Scrapple." *Philadelphia Inquirer,* April 16, 1991. Obituary of E. Harper Habbersett, with a brief history of the family business.

Cook's Corner. "Oatmeal Scrapple." *Columbus Dispatch*, January 3, 2001.

Graeff, Arthur D. "Dickens and Panhass." *Morning Call* (Allentown, PA), September 28, 1946.

Gray, Christopher. "New York's First Automat." *New York Times,* June 30, 1991. A history of the Horn & Hardart automats in New York.

Hanania, Joseph. "Tales of a Great Marketplace." *Today/Philadelphia Inquirer,* April 24, 1977, 12–15. Traces the attempted revitalization of the Reading Terminal Market.

"How to Make Scrapple: Indians Gave First Recipe to Pennsylvania Dutch." *Evening Bulletin* (Philadelphia), November 23, 1964. The article claims that the Native Americans gave the Pennsylvania Dutch the word *Panhas* and used bear and venison. The recipe supplied is flavored with poultry seasoning.

Jacobs, Carole, and Michael Rellahan. "Strode's Plant Sold to Lebanon Firm." *Daily Local News* (West Chester, PA), June 3, 1983.

Land, Leslie. "Sampling Scrapple at the Source." *New York Times,* April 5, 1987. Good roundup of local producers, plus an interview with William Woys Weaver and a photograph of scrapple at the Melrose Diner in Philadelphia.

Lowry, Don. "Links to Success," *Savannah Morning News,* June 30, 2001. Deals with Ratchford's Market in Guyton, Georgia.

Purvis, Kathleen. "Welcome to Livermush Land." *Charlotte Observer,* October 18, 2000.

"Scrapple Is Plain—But Tasty." *Philadelphia Inquirer,* October 4, 1972.

"Scrapple? You're Talking Real Penna Dutch Delicacies!" *Lancaster New Era,* September 17, 1984. The focus is on Youndt Brothers, country butchers at Denver, Pennsylvania, north of Lancaster.

Smart, James. "In Our Town." *Evening Bulletin* (Philadelphia), March 20, 1962. Mentions A. Darlington Strode's canned scrapple.

Socca, Tom. "You Gonna Eat That?" *Baltimore Citypaper,* February 23–29, 2000.

"A Tribute to Francis Strode." *Daily Local News* (West Chester, PA), May 7, 1890.

Manuscripts

Hickman, Esther Hannum. "Household Receipts." Dugdale (Pennsbury Township), Chester County, PA, begun 1881. Roughwood Collection.

Hill, Lizzie W. "Lizzie W. Hill's Account Book." Begun November 25, 1874. Collection of the Chester County Historical Society, West Chester, PA.

Recipe Book, Manuscript (1840–1900). Lancaster County, PA. Ms. Codex 800. Collection of the Rare Book and Manuscript Division, Van Pelt Library, University of Pennsylvania, Philadelphia.

Rhoads, Rebecca. "Diary." Philadelphia, 1831–57. Five volumes with entries in reused cash books from the firm Rhoads & Hancock. Rhoads was a Quaker and a member of Green Street Meeting in Philadelphia. She was a friend of Quaker confectioner Hannah Widdifield. Roughwood Collection.

Interviews

Lauterbach, Margaret. January 11, 2001. Interview about venison scrapple and life in eastern Colorado during the early 1900s.

Mumper, Benjamin. May 3, 1986. Interview about butchering practices at New Germantown, Perry County, Pennsylvania, especially directions for making pudding meat.

Polk, Evangeline ("Evelina"). December 28, 2002. Interview concerning liver mush and poor-do. Born "about 1924," Polk grew up in Pike County, Kentucky.

Weaver, Grace Hickman. July 20, 1983. Interview concerning scrapple production at the farm of her father William E. Hickman, Pocopson, Chester County, Pennsylvania, prior to 1912.

———. July 5, 1991. Interview concerning the production of stuffed hams, which her father sold at the West Chester Farmers' Market.

Zimmerman, L. Wilbur. November 26, 2001. Interview concerning pot pudding and ham scrapple at Mount Holly Springs, Cumberland County, Pennsylvania, prior to 1920.

INDEX